THE HOW AND WHY OF HOME SCHOOLING

The How and Why of Home Schooling

Ray E. Ballmann

CROSSWAY BOOKS • WHEATON, ILLINOIS
A DIVISION OF GOOD NEWS PUBLISHERS

Cover Illustration by Jesse Willcox Smith, 1909, from "The Seven Ages of Childhood."

Cover and book design by Karen L. Mulder

First printing, 1987

Printed in the United States of America

Library of Congress Catalog Card Number 86-72263

ISBN 0-89107-425-2

Biblical quotations, unless otherwise indicated, are taken from *Holy Bible: New International Version*, copyright © 1978 by the New York International Bible Society. Used by permission of Zondervan Bible Publishers.

01	00	99	98	97	96	95	94
11	10	9	8	7	6		

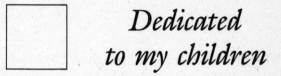

Dedicated
to my children

TABLE OF
Contents

Acknowledgments

The author gratefully acknowledges those who graciously gave of their time and energies to the completion of this book. Special thanks is due my wife, Cindy, for her many hours of help and support; to Gregg Harris and Jan Dennis for their editorial suggestions; and to Richard Stimson for his word processing assistance. In addition, appreciation is due Dr. Raymond Moore for his outstanding research and great pioneering efforts in the field of home education.

Foreword

With so many young families rediscovering the educational potential of their own homes, there has been an explosion of new books on home schooling. Like the rediscovery of home cooking, home-based education is making many parents wonder why anyone would ever choose anything else. And, just as with cooking, there are many how-to books to choose from. Why should anyone read Ray Ballmann's new book? Where does it fit into the picture?

By and large, home-schooled children are healthier kids, with a better understanding of their studies, greater respect for their elders, greater social skills, and a better outlook on life than their age-mates in the public or even the private schools. That is why home schooling is a growing movement in the educational community.

The How & Why of Home Schooling is a book designed to *provoke* Christian parents to a very good work—the work of teaching children at home—and then to *equip* them for that work. In addition to arming his readers with strong, Biblically illuminated arguments for *why* you should not put your children in the public school, Ray offers excellent guidelines on *how* to actually teach your child successfully at home.

The public schools have become, in effect, the parochial schools of secular humanism. This has been accomplished in the twentieth century by the gradual transformation of every state teacher's college in the U.S. into a virtual seminary of secular humanism. The public school classroom is the vacation Bible school, the Sunday school, and the pulpit of a nontheistic but no less dogmatic New Age religion. Education in America is an act of religious warfare.

Ray's book may seem combative at points to those who are used to the more positive attitudes of the typical Christian home schooler. Having known Ray for some time, I can confidently say that he is as positive as anyone could be about his experience in teaching his children at home. That comes through in his how-to section. But Ray is also an experienced pastor and Bible teacher who recognizes a religious battle when he sees one. He has good reason to be combative. And when you must be combative, you might as well go for a knockout. That, in my opinion, is where this volume fits into the growing body of home school literature.

It is a knockout.

Gregg Harris
Author/Instructor of *The Home Schooling Workshop*
March 1987

ONE

Home Schooling: The Return of A Biblical Model Of Education

H ome schooling is destined to become one of the most exciting and explosive movements of the eighties and nineties. Already it is the signpost of a profound social and educational shift at the grass-roots level. Public education has for years been losing its glitter, and even now its fractured foundation is crumbling on every side. In the wake of massive youth illiteracy, immorality, and rebellion against domestic authority, concerned parents all across America are exercising their right to teach their children at home. Hence, the thriving home schooling movement has become one of the most encouraging and hope-inspiring developments in our country today.

Perhaps, like many people today, you are asking, "What is home schooling all about? Are those who home school part of a lunatic fringe of society, consisting of a mixture of fanatics, radicals and escapists? Or is it a legitimate movement? Why are people in growing numbers starting to home school?" These are legitimate questions. It is my hope that these and other questions will be answered in the pages that follow. If you have an interest in knowing more about the emergence, growth, and purpose of the home schooling movement, this book was written with you especially in mind. Further, I hope to demonstrate why *you* should personally consider home schooling and how to begin.

Some of the greatest names in history were educated at

home. Home schooling has helped forge some of the world's best leaders, writers, and inventors—exceptional men and women with sound character, emotional stability, and intellectual genius. Here is a partial list of those who have been educated at home or who have been privately tutored.

Abigail Adams	Douglas MacArthur
John Quincy Adams	James Madison
Hans Christian Andersen	Cyrus McCormick
Alexander Graham Bell	John Stuart Mill
Pearl Buck	Claude Monet
Andrew Carnegie	James Monroe
George Washington Carver	Wolfgang Mozart
Charlie Chaplin	Blaise Pascal
Agatha Christie	George Patton
Winston Churchill	William Penn
George Rogers Clark	Franklin Delano Roosevelt
Noel Coward	Theodore Roosevelt
Pierre Curie	George Bernard Shaw
Charles Dickens	Albert Schweitzer
Pierre DuPont	Leo Tolstoy
Thomas Edison	Mark Twain
Albert Einstein	George Washington
Benjamin Franklin	Martha Washington
Alexander Hamilton	Daniel Webster
Bret Harte	John Wesley
Patrick Henry	Phyllis Wheatley
Stonewall Jackson	Woodrow Wilson
Robert E. Lee	Orville Wright
Abraham Lincoln	Wilbur Wright
C. S. Lewis	Andrew Wyeth[1]

Humanistic contingents, liberal elements in the educational bureaucracy, and the uninformed have charged that home schoolers comprise a lunatic fringe of society. But the history of our nation clearly demonstrates otherwise. Home schoolers constitute the very flower of human potential, leadership, and ability. Most of those listed were persons of compassion, intelligence, skill, adeptness, and self-sufficiency. And the common root which cultivated these unique qualities was home tutoring.

Until just after World War I, family schools were the principal form of education in America. The home served as the social center of influence, the root of moral and spiritual guidance, and the primary academic instructor. The only exceptions to this general rule were during those periods following major wars or immediately prior to societal collapse when child education was largely given over to slaves or public agencies. The chilling consequences of these exceptional times were that children grew up without having received a solid base of values and morality. Hence, after 1812, 1865, 1918, and 1945 the United States suffered from epidemic crime and moral breakdown.[2] Today once again public institutions have begun to replace the home in vital areas, often becoming the predominant source of forming and transmitting values in our nation's youth, with the same devastating results.

The following succinct review of American education shows a slow cancerous growth of anti-Christian philosophies in the school system, along with the appropriate response by concerned Christian families nationwide.

1620—Christian education. Schools taught the Bible and colleges like Harvard, Princeton, and Yale were founded to train young men to preach the gospel.

1837—public education begins. The first public school was established. Horace Mann, a Unitarian, worked for a state-controlled educational system. The Bible was still taught in the public schools.

1905—progressive education. John Dewey, the father of progressive education, introduced Socialistic, anti-Christian philosophy in the schools. The Bible was separated from academic studies.

1933—humanistic education. The Humanist Manifesto written by John Dewey and thirty-three other signers enunciates the doctrines of secular humanism. God and the supernatural are rejected and replaced with man's reason and science.

1963—anti-Christian education. Bible reading in public schools is declared unconstitutional. The vacuum is quickly filled with curriculum materials that promote immorality, rebellion against parents, the occult, and other teachings contrary to Scripture.

1965—rise of Christian education. There are now over ten thousand Christian schools to combat the destructive education of religious humanism. A Christian school is started every seven hours.[3]

1980s—rise of home education. Desiring to return to the Biblical model, concerned parents all across America begin reclaiming their right and responsibility for the education of their children. Home schooling is now active in all fifty states, with participating families currently estimated at over one million.

We must ask ourselves, Why has public education been largely taken over by proponents of anti-Christian, antifamily values? The answer is obvious. Education is the means by which the next generation forms its outlook on the world. Young hearts and minds are especially vulnerable, and if those opposed to Christianity can capture the educational strongholds, they can go a long way toward molding the next generation in their own image.

But the jig is up. More and more parents—Christians and non-Christians alike—concerned with preserving and transmitting traditional moral and educational values are opting out of the public schools. The home school movement is a direct consequence of the increasing de-Christianization of our nation's classrooms and textbooks combined with the secular world view which already saturates the American educational process. Concerned parents have become outraged at today's appalling educational environment. Hence, in a massive protest against the public schools, they are pulling their children out and saying, "Enough is enough." At the same time they are rediscovering their own educational calling. Vigilant Christian parents in all fifty states are responding to the numerous Biblical injunctions which make them ultimately accountable for child training and instruction.

Growing numbers of Christian parents are refusing to lay back in docile compliance to the massive public educational system. No longer are they recoiling in intimidation and fear or waffling helplessly in uncertainty of action. Instead, many are beginning to fight back. They are putting on their spiritual armor and hoisting the battle flag for combat and struggle "against the rulers, against the authorities, against the powers of this world and against the spiritual forces of evil in the heavenly realms" (Eph. 6:12). Many are retaking the mantle of educational duties upon themselves and forging ahead into victory for their children.

There are several reasons why Christian parents across our land are starting to home school. First and foremost is the fact that the Bible states that educational responsibility lies firmly in parental hands. Deuteronomy 6 is one of the many Biblical passages that explicate the child-rearing and education responsibilities of parents. Parents must see to it that their children are taught the Word of God in its fullness and purity. Balanced education cannot take place in a spiritual vacuum. This is one of several areas where public education failed and failed miserably. There is no such thing as academic neutrality. True education integrates faith in Jesus Christ and the content and process of learning. True education seeks to train not just the mind but also the heart and soul.

This is what we call character training. Development of

character is critical to the proper growth and maturation of a young child. Home educators are returning to the crucial development and nurture of character. The most important task of the educator is to prepare his students for life. And the best way to prepare a student for life is to teach, model, and promote the development of godly character. Character training is the most important and most laudable activity for a teacher to be engaged in. If a student is taught nothing else save character alone, he will be better prepared for life than those who are taught pure academics but no character. Commenting on the absence of character training in American schools, child-development expert Dr. Urie Bronfenbrenner says:

> In terms of content, education in America, when viewed from a cross-cultural perspective, seems peculiarly one-sided, emphasizing subject matter to the exclusion of another fundamental aspect of the child's development for which there is no generally accepted term in our educational vocabulary: what the Germans call *erziehung*, the Russians *vospitanie* and the French *éducation*. Perhaps the best equivalents are "upbringing" or "character education," expressions that sound outmoded and irrelevant to us. In many countries of Western and Eastern Europe, however, the corresponding terms are the names of what constitutes the core of the educational process: the development of the child's qualities as a person—his values, motives, and patterns of social response.[4]

Should not this be the core of American education as well? Christian parents understand exactly the missing element that Dr. Bronfenbrenner speaks about. It is the essential qualities so grieviously lacking in many young people today. It is the teaching and development of Christlike qualities such as love, kindness, forgiveness, honesty, service, dependence on God, enthusiasm/hunger for the Word of God, and prayer. It is also the nurturing of highly valued practical virtues such as cleanliness, dependability, neatness, and hard work. Students who are taught these qualities will more likely become the future leaders and model citizens of our society. They will exhibit traits such as industry and ingenuity instead of laziness and negligence, self-leading and independence instead of peer-manipulation and control, giving instead of taking, serving instead of always being served. This, in turn, will go a long way toward giving the child a sense of high self-respect and purpose for living. Are these not the qualities every responsible parent wants to see in his or her child? Because of the environmental conditions and consistent modeling opportunities unique to home educators, parents can successfully take advantage of building godly character in their child.

There is only one way American youth can remain morally and spiritually undaunted, and that is to be in constant contact with the Word of God. When confronted with the Scriptural interrogative, "How can a young man keep his way pure?" parents and Christian educators take refuge in the solution divinely provided: "By living according to your word" (Ps. 119:9). But if the purifying light and influence of God's Word is removed from public classrooms, as it has been done, then humanistic forces have gained the upper hand. Wise Christian parents do not ignore this fact and hide their heads in the sand. Instead, they seriously examine their educational alternatives. And one of the solutions many have arrived at is home schooling, which is a return to a Biblical model of education.

TWO

Is Home Schooling For You?

onsider seriously these questions. Do you believe that your child is a gift of God and your greatest earthly blessing? Do you want the very best that life has to offer your child? Do you cherish your child's love, attention, and respect? Are you interested in discovering that essential "missing ingredient" that is lacking in so many families today? Are you concerned about the present course of public education in America? Is the development of your child's moral character, academic competency, responsibility, discipline, and social grace important to you? Are you concerned about your child's spiritual growth? Do you want your child to be a winner in life? Finally, are you open to explore a very old and yet startlingly new concept in alternative education? If so, then perhaps *you* are a prime candidate for home schooling.

For too long now parental value and worth have been belittled by antifamily interest groups. Over the years parents have been deceptively led to believe that they are unqualified to teach and unable to adequately impart sound values. Parents have been made to feel inept in every way when it comes to educating their own children. A barrage of disinformation from antifamily proponents, the educational establishment, and the media has reinforced these views. As a result, parents have slowly come to believe that public schools can do a far better job than they can of instructing and instilling values in their children.

This is simply not so. The truth is, if you are a responsible, loving, and concerned parent, you not only qualify to raise your child but to teach him as well.

Is home schooling for *you*? The answer to that question is a resounding yes if you agree with five basic convictions. These convictions are enunciated below in the form of five questions.

Conviction #1

Do you believe that God and patriotism should still hold a vital place in the classroom? What used to be commonplace is now considered taboo. Because of a mounting anti-Christian, antipatriotic bias which has covertly infiltrated our public schools, many complain that God has been ousted and patriotism belittled. President Reagan recently said, "The God who blessed us with life, gave us knowledge, and made us good and caring people should never have been expelled from our schools."[1] How far we have come indeed when the President of the United States must acknowledge the expulsion of God in our public schools. I remember the days when my public high school said the Pledge of Allegiance and had a brief devotion led by the student council each morning. Those days are gone and now even *voluntary* prayer is judicially forbidden.

A recent Gallup Poll shows that seven in ten Americans favor school prayer.[2] Unfortunately, the most we have is an "equal access" law (passed July 25, 1984), whose interpretation and application has left much to be desired. Equally lamentable, the Pledge of Allegiance is infrequently or never spoken in many classrooms today. When God and country mean so much to the majority of Americans, why can't these essentials be maintained daily in every classroom in the country?

Is there anything more important to your child than his spiritual development and maturation? Not if your priorities are right! The Bible says, "Seek *first* [God's] kingdom and his righteousness, and all these things will be given to you" (Matt. 6:33). What shapes your child's development more than his daily environment? It is not as though our public classrooms are godless; it's just that they have been *replaced* with a different god—the god of this world. Love of God has been substituted with self-centeredness and worldly, antifamily values. Traditional morality is largely ignored, while immorality is condoned. Regrettably, the cancerous anti-Christian sentiment prevalent in many public schools today is demoralizing the soul of millions of our young children.

Mel and Norma Gabler, specialists in critiquing public school textbooks, have found that much public school literature follows "depressive, negative themes." Below are twelve categories of negative themes they have found nationwide in textbook reviews.

1) Alienation
2) Death and suicide
3) Degradation or humiliation
4) Depression
5) Discontentment
6) Fear and horror

7) Hate
8) Disrespect
9) Low goals
10) Lack of motivation
11) Problems stressed
12) Skepticism[3]

Are these the themes that come from an all-loving God? Do they build and promote godly character and self-esteem, or do they destroy it? Why do these pervasive themes appear to run through the heart of our public school textbooks? How can a Christian foundation be fostered with such literature being shoved down the throats of our children? A recent study by professor Paul Vitz of New York University proves conclusively that the textbooks typically used in public education exclude Christianity and traditional values. Vitz writes:

> Are public school textbooks biased? Are they censored? The answer to both is yes. And the nature of the bias is clear: Religion, traditional family values, and conservative political and economic positions have been reliably excluded from children's textbooks. This exclusion is particularly disturbing because it is found in a system paid for by taxpayers and one that claims, moreover, to be committed to impartial knowledge and accuracy.[4]

It is not just the textbooks, either. This anti-Christian bias has invaded and polluted every arena of the school system with its vicious poison. Without a doubt, God and traditional morality have been forced out the front school door.

Another exclusionary tactic seems evident when it comes to patriotism. It shows itself not only in what is *said*, but also in what is being *left unsaid*. Some textbooks are silent about the heroic efforts of brave new men in American history, as we shall see in Chapter 3. These same texts frequently overlook facts which build patriotism and national pride, the bedrock of our freedom and democracy. A proper love of country seems absent among many of today's youth. Why aren't the Pledge of Allegiance and patriotism in general more prominent in many of our classrooms?

It is my firm conviction that God and patriotism *belong* in the classroom. All the home schooling families I know cherish their national and religious heritage and endeavor to impart that same knowledge to their children. How important is it to you?

Conviction #2

Is the development and growth of your child's delicate self-respect very important to you? Of course it is! This is one area where home schooling can excel. Many parents feel the battle for healthy self-respect is being waged in the school classroom and is being lost. Every year thousands of young, impressionable children are being sacrificed to the beast of insensitivity. The powerful public educational system feeds this beast daily with a growing diet of immoral, violence-prone, antifamily textbooks coupled with a side dish of behavior modification and value clarification techniques. Add to this a daily seasoning of worldly peer pressure, and what do you have? A confused child with a mounting self-image problem. Worse yet, by the time it becomes noticeable, irreparable damage has most likely occurred.

Your child's self-respect is a key to his success in life. His whole personality and effectiveness in the future is made or broken within the confines of his self-image. It is a child's self-respect that makes him view the world as either cold and cruel or challenging and adventuresome. A healthy self-respect is one of the most priceless gifts that you can help your child develop.

A comprehensive study of self-respect was carried out by Dr. Stanley Coopersmith. The conclusion of this intensive study revealed that parents have a powerful influence on a child's self-image. Parents can give their child the ability to withstand societal pressure by bolstering his confidence, or they can leave him practically defenseless. How parents respond and interact with their growing child will mold him one way or the other. A child who feels the warmth, love, attention, and respect of his parents will most likely grow up with a high degree of self-worth. Says Dr. Coopersmith:

> Children—young children especially—are vulnerable and dependent upon their parents . . . they survive and thrive largely by accommodating themselves to parental standards. . . . Parental acceptance has an enhancing effect upon self-esteem in particular, and psychosocial development in general. Parental rejection, the other extreme, presumably results in an impoverished environment and a diminished sense of personal worthiness.[5]

Who is more concerned about your child's self-image than you are? No one! On occasion there may be individual teachers who show a special interest in their students, but rarely as comprehensively as a loving mother and father. Concerned parents are the *crucial* element in a child's emotional development. Mom and Dad, *no one* can build your child's self-esteem or prepare him for life quite like you.

Conviction #3

Do you want to continue a special bond of closeness between you and your child? Every loving and discerning parent does. Yet, beginning with a child's first year away in school, a distancing often develops between a parent and child, and it can increase every year your child remains in the public system. It may be unnoticable at first, but as the years go by a rebellious, antiparent, philosophical indoctrination will reveal its indelible mark.

Here is the sad part. In spite of the overwhelming propaganda to the contrary, a child need not be kicked out of his loving nest at age five to be "socialized."

Speaking on the topic of children being sent off to school at an early age, Dr. Raymond Moore asserts:

> It is as if they were little birds fallen or pushed out of the nest before they were ready—frantically, fearfully fluttering around on the ground, unable to make the fullest use of their beautiful but unready wings.
>
> At early school they soon find that they must compete for teacher approval, instead of having instant recourse to Mother or Daddy. They must compete for toys often before they are emotionally able or ready to share. And perhaps worst of all, turned out by their parents, they begin quickly to compete for the attention of their age-mates, absorb their language and manners and habits and mores, and become dependent on their approval.
>
> When parents try to explain why children should not say certain things, they may not understand, for they are not yet consistently reasonable, or "cognitively ready"—they do not understand fully the "why" of Mother's or Daddy's explanation. And since "all the kids are doing it," they give the backs of their little hands to their parents' cherished values, and become dependent upon their peers for their value systems. Thus step by step *parents lose control, their authority usurped by the school authorities* to whom they delegated responsibility for their children.[6]

Home schooled children have a unique bond of closeness with their parents. The reason is that they have spent priceless time being nurtured by a physical, emotional, and spiritual closeness to Mom and Dad. And that bonding also extends to sibling relationships. Brothers and sisters are closer and have deeper interrelationships when they are home schooled. Because they share more childhood experiences apart from school peer pressure, they develop a refreshing dependence on the family. Futurist Alvin Toffler touches on this in his book *The Third Wave* where he suggests home schooling as a sane response to mass education and an excellent way to restore community and family life.

Peer pressure at an early age should be of grave concern to parents. In elementary years in particular, a child is not mature enough to develop values independently. He struggles to find an example, someone to give him desperately needed guidance. He looks for a model in the one thing available in quantity, his school environment. Unfortunately, it is difficult for him to delineate between right and wrong. Further still, he is extremely susceptible to the mannerisms, language, attitudes, and values of his age-mates. Since he is not old enough to resist ridicule from those he works and plays with, he unknowingly caves into peer conformity. This, in turn, weakens the parental bonds and values cherished and loved by so many.

Conviction #4

As a parent, do you have more of your child's best interest at heart that any one else? Your answer to this question is of paramount importance. Most parents believe they have more of their child's best interest at heart than a nine-month-a-year public education teacher. One reason is that a teacher's student interest can wax and wane with mood, group size, and classroom conditions. This mood can change day to day, week to week, and year to year. Usually a teacher must develop rapport not only with a new class, but with each individual child as well. This would be a monumental undertaking for even the best professional psychiatrist, much less a teacher. But the real question is: how can such educational transience serve the young child's best instructional and emotional interest?

Even if rapport is built, a further question must be raised. How much individual attention does the average teacher give to his students? How many teachers take time to meet each child's personal requirements? Dr. John Goodlad, graduate dean of education at UCLA, did a comparative study of over a thousand schools and found that the average amount of time spent in one-on-one responses between teachers and students amounted to "seven minutes a day."[7] How much individual attention can a child receive in seven minutes a day? Certainly there are dedicated teachers who have a genuine interest in their students, but how many? And for those who do not, how will the child's desperate need for recognition and self-approval be fulfilled? Without question, there is no replacement for personal attention to young, emotionally delicate students.

A renowned expert in the area of home schooling is developmental psychologist Dr. Raymond Moore. Dr. Moore has made the following vital observations in the area of classroom deficiency.

> In the typical school, children cannot be treated with partiality—individually or personally—but only as integral part of the class. In spite of the fact that children of the same age vary greatly in ability, achievement, background, and personality, they must more or less go through the same assembly line—doing the same thing at the same time and fitting roughly into the same mold as the others. In truth, the partiality needed by the young child brings the feeling that he is special to his parents—loved and cherished as a unique individual. These forced omissions and most schools' overwhelming concern for subject matter greatly interfere with free exploration and the child's development as a unique person.
>
> Contrast the school routine with the opportunities your youngster has in a reasonably well-regulated, loving home. Here he experiences relative quiet and simplicity in his daily program; one-to-one responses to his questions, needs, and interest, practically on call; and the opportunity for solitude. As he is allowed to associate closely with his parents in their daily activities of work, play, rest, and conversation, the child shares responsibility and feels that he is part of the family team—needed, wanted, and depended upon. And thereby he develops a sense of self-worth, the cornerstone of positive socialization.[8]

Dr. Moore further states:

> For the first eight to ten years at least—until their values are formed, most parents, even average parents, are by far

the best people for their children. And those that are not, usually can and should be. . . . Most mothers and fathers can provide deeper security, sheerer closeness, sharper instincts, longer continuity, warmer responses, more logical control and more natural examples than the staff of the best care center or kindergarten.[9]

Dr. David Elkind in his book *The Hurried Child* notes this shocking description of the modern public school classroom:

> Little time is given to actual instruction in classrooms. Management, busywork, waiting, leaving and arriving, and other diversions reduce gross instructional time to around ninety minutes a day. . . . In class, attention to single students may average, per student, only six hours per year.
>
> To "cover the material," teachers need response from students able and willing to give it, and so they pay attention to about a third of the class, largely ignoring those who need instruction most, who may be written off as "failures" in the early weeks of the semester. A high percentage of failures is expected and accepted.[10]

There are some things about your child only you as a parent can know. For example, your child might be in a poor frame of mind for learning if his dog died the night before. Knowing this will help you as a parent to be more understanding of your child's emotional requirements. Only a parent knows that his child's eating habits have dropped off, or that he has been preoccupied with some physical defect or condition and is supersensitive to ridicule. Only a parent can truly know his child's heart and be concerned about it.

Unquestionably the interest that you as a parent have in your child not only has the weightier motivation of parental love and affection, but it also spans a more diverse spectrum of overall concern. Instead of being concerned primarily with a child's mental development, a godly parent is also concerned with his child's physical, psychological, emotional, and spiritual well-being.

Conviction #5

Are you willing to embrace your parental and constitutional rights? Scripture charges parents with educational accountability for how and what their children are taught. Parents are to be the key educational superintendent of their children. This is more than just a privilege; it is a Scriptural injunction of sweeping magnitude. Children are a gift of God placed completely under parental charge. Holy Writ gives parents the educational reins. What you do with those reins is an awesome responsibility.

Beyond this, the Constitution of the United States along with its amendments guarantees every citizen certain inalienable rights. One of those rights is the freedom to teach your own children because of religious convictions. This is a fundamental constitutional right. Regarding parental liberty, the Supreme Court in *Yoder* tenaciously held:

> This case involves the fundamental interest of parents, as contrasted with that of the state, to guide the religious future and *education of their children*. The history and culture of Western civilization reflect a strong tradition of parental concern for the nurture and upbringing of their children. This primary role of the parents in the upbringing of their children is now *established beyond debate as an enduring American tradition.* . . .
>
> The fundamental theory of liberty upon which all governments in this union repose excludes any general power of the state to standardize its children by forcing them to accept instruction from public teachers only. The child is not the mere creature of the state; those who nurture him and direct his destiny have the right, coupled with the high duty, to recognize and prepare him for additional obligations.[11] (emphasis mine)

In 1986, U.S. Secretary of Education William J. Bennett wrote:

> The child, the Supreme Court made clear in *Pierce v. Society of Sisters* (1925), "is not the mere creature of the state." Today more than ever we need to empower parents with respect to the education of their children. This must include affording them an array of alternatives—and holding them accountable for choosing wisely.[12]

In these days of big government, with its ever-expanding power and influence over family life, free citizens must guard their constitutional rights with utmost care. Infringement of your precious rights may be taking place right now. History vividly records how easy it is to lose them.

If you answered the majority of the above questions *yes*, then home schooling could very well be for you. Home schoolers are not odd, but they are different in that they desire to raise their children with a radical view of life, a godly one! They choose morality, intelligence, and family commitment instead of the present societal mold of depravity, ignorance, and peer dependency. They want to be close to their children throughout all their growing years. They do not want to wake up one day and find out they are strangers to their own children. This is often the regrettable plight of well-intentioned parents. Could this happen to you? It certainly could! How? By allowing a slow but deeply instilled rebellious spirit to be seeded and nurtured in your child in the classrooms. Those who think it could never happen to them are usually the same ones who are indifferent to what their children are being taught. Loving parents want children who have abiding values and respect for life. But this is not automatic. It only comes to those who are willing to affirm both their parental and constitutional rights and exercise them. It comes to those who are willing to pay the price and invest their time in their greatest earthly gift: their children.

How about you? What kind of children do you want to raise? What do you desire them to be like in five years? In ten? In fifteen? The law of the farmer applies: you reap what you sow. If you let the world feed, water, and cultivate your child, expect the appropriate results. If you entrust your child for seven hours a day, five days a week, into a conventional school setting, expect him to absorb and emulate his environment. But remember this, your child's delicate spirit and personality are entrusted to your care for only a brief time, and then the opportunity is gone. I know of no better way to develop and nurture an endearing relationship with your child than through home schooling. What kind of child do you want to raise?

Summary

If you can share the following five convictions, then home schooling may very well be *right for you*. 1) I believe that God and patriotism should still hold a vital place in the classroom. 2) The development and growth of my child's fragile self-respect is very important to me. 3) I want to continue a special bond of closeness between me and my child. 4) As a parent, I have more of my child's best interest at heart than anyone else. 5) I am willing to embrace both my parental (in light of Scripture) and constitutional rights.

THREE

Public Education: The Assault on Excellence

I n this chapter we want to take a hard but realistic look at public education as it is today. In order to do this objectively, we must shed our skins of defensiveness and fear. We must not try to excuse or rationalize any failures of the system that we may uncover. The time has arrived to remove the fog and see the system for what it really is. Nostalgic views of yesteryear's public school do not apply. As long as we do not project our perception of the past into the present, it is all right to reminisce. But we must keep in mind that what may have been true then is probably not true today.

Report Card on Public Education

There are those who ask, "Why should we be so concerned about public education and its direction? Why not let the educators handle their own problems?" There are at least three good reasons why we should concern ourselves with public education.

First, public education is extremely expensive. It digs deeply into the pockets of our working population. Taxpayers do not want to see their hard-earned dollars squandered. They have a right to want a good return on their educational investment (some $230 billion in 1983). Considering that public education is "the second-largest industry in America, with 2.3 million classroom teachers; the largest union in the world; and the second-largest budget in government (second only to the welfare department),"[1] why is it doing a second-rate job?

□ *29*

Second, we should be concerned because many of the recent products of our educational system are apparently illiterate and ill-equipped to handle even the most basic demands of life. Jonathan Kozol, in his book *Illiterate America*, draws our attention to these appalling facts:

Twenty-five million adults cannot read the poison warnings on a can of pesticide, a letter from their child's teacher, or the front page of a daily paper. An additional 35 million read only at a level which is less than equal to the full survival needs of our society. Together, these 60 million people represent more than one third of the entire population. . . .

Given a paycheck and the stub that lists the usual deductions, 26 percent of adult Americans cannot determine if their paycheck is correct. Thirty-six percent, given a W-4 form, cannot enter the right number of exemptions in the proper places on the form. Forty-four percent, when given a series of "Help Wanted" ads, cannot match their qualifications to the job requirements. Twenty-two percent cannot address a letter well enough to guarantee that it will reach its destination. Twenty-four percent cannot add their own correct return address to the same envelope. Twenty percent cannot understand an "Equal Opportunity" announcement. Over 60 percent, given a series of "For Sale" advertisements for products new and used, cannot calculate the difference between prices for a new and used appliance. Over 20 percent cannot write a check that will be processed by their bank—or will be processed in the right amount. Over 40 percent are unable to determine the correct amount of change they should receive, given a cash register receipt and the denomination of the bill used for payment.[2]

That our schools are in trouble is an open fact. A briefing paper prepared by the educational testing service for the United States Department of Education exclaims:

In 1983, eight major national studies reported on the status of public education in the United States. These reports sounded a common theme: *"The American educational system is in trouble."*[3] (emphasis mine)

With results like this coming out of our public schools, how can any loyal American not be concerned? If this trend continues, where will our nation be in a few short years? Students who graduate illiterate and ill-equipped to face life not only hurt themselves, but they also adversely affect those around them.

We should be gravely concerned about a faltering educational system because American society pays a very high price. When I speak of price, I am not referring here to money we spend on education, but rather the cost to our country in those things which are often intangible and yet essential. For example, illiteracy robs our citizenry of the ability to understand and analyze current events. "Forty-five percent of adult citizens do not read newspapers. Only 10 percent abstain by choice. The rest have been excluded by their inability to read."[4] Newspapers are already written on an estimated tenth grade level, but even that crutch is unable to save those who cannot read.

Our society pays dearly in other areas too. It exacts a heavy toll on defense posture and military readiness. For example:

> Thirty percent of naval recruits were recently termed "a danger to themselves and to costly naval equipment" because of inability to read and understand instructions. The Navy reports that one recruit caused $250,000 in damage to delicate equipment "because he could not read the repair manual.". . . How many more illiterates are now responsible for lower-level but essential safety checks that are required in handling of missiles or the operation of a nuclear reactor? . . .
>
> Books resembling comics are one of the common methods of instruction. A five-page picture book is needed to explain the steps required to release and lift the hood of army vehicles."[5]

Illiteracy and academic inferiority affect our ability to compete in international markets. They affect our productivity. Already there are growing complaints that we can't keep up with foreign competition in steel, automobiles, electronics, optics, textiles, and other key areas. These grave educational deficiencies affect an individual's self-esteem and his hopes of "getting ahead." The cost of inadequately educating our future leaders, scientists, mathematicians, and our workforce in general is indeed high. A sound education is essential to our country's health and well-being. Americans know this to be true; that is why they feel that public education contributes more to national strength than either industrial might or military power.[6]

Parents in ever increasing numbers are responding defensively to protect their children from wave after wave of school-generated problems, ungodly peer pressures, and foundering educational standards. But why should they be forced into a defensive posture when their children are in tax-supported institutions? This is one of the regrettable ironies of modern education in America.

What is going on in our public schools today? That is the crucial question at hand concerning public education. As we dive into some of the facts, let's remember that we are not embarking on some kind of an antipublic school campaign. Our objective here is personal enlightenment of what is currently taking place in many of our public schools. Then, after we analyze the facts, we want to ask ourselves: Is public school where I want my child to be? What are my educational alternatives? More specifically, is home schooling a viable option for me?

Now, if we were to evaluate the public school system today and give it a report card, it might look something like this.

F in Academics

F in Morality

F in Student Self-Image

F in Discipline

F in Patriotism

As we consider each of these areas one by one, ask yourself, Is this the environment I really want my child in?

F in Academics

The failure of our public school system in the area of academics is both regrettable and unnecessary. Why should the children of America, who live in the greatest and most powerful nation on earth, be sinking to the bottom of the academic barrel? There is no justifiable excuse for the fact that the United States ranks forty-ninth among 158 member nations of the U.N. in its literacy levels.[7] An article in the *Dallas Morning News* (August 26, 1971) was entitled "Young People Are Getting Dumber." In this article, the director of Human Engineering Laboratory said that young people today know less than their parents. The director went on to explain that they have recorded a 1 percent drop in vocabulary per year. Consider the devastating impact. It doesn't take much to figure out what a drop in knowledge of 1 percent a year for thirty years will do to America.

The academic decline in America has not gone unnoticed. U.S. Senator Samuel I. Hayakawa warned the Senate back in 1978 that schools have become vehicles for a "heresy that rejects the idea of education as the acquisition of knowledge and skills" and instead "regards the fundamental task in education as therapy."[8] In 1983 the National Commission on Excellence in Education gave its report to Congress. Among other things, it revealed the following shocking facts about the academic environment in America:

> Our society and its educational institutions seem to have lost sight of the basic purposes of schooling, and of the high expectations and disciplined effort needed to attain them. . . .
>
> International comparisons of student achievement, completed a decade ago, reveal that on 19 academic tests American students were never first or second and, in comparison with other industrialized nations, were last seven times.
>
> Some 23 million American adults are functionally illiterate by the simplest tests of everyday reading, writing, and comprehension.
>
> About 13 percent of all 17-year-olds in the United States can be considered functionally illiterate. Functional illiteracy among minority youth may run as high as 40 percent.
>
> Average achievement of high school students on most standardized tests is now lower than 26 years ago when Sputnik was launched.
>
> The College Board's Scholastic Aptitude Tests (SAT) demonstrate a virtually unbroken decline from 1963 to 1980. Average verbal scores fell over 50 points and average mathematics scores dropped nearly 40 points.[9]

Not only is Congress aware of this academic decline, but so are some top education professionals. Declares John I. Goodlad, former dean of the UCLA Graduate school of Education, after completing an eight-year study: "American schools are in trouble. In fact, the problems of schooling are of such crippling proportions that many schools may not survive. It is possible that our entire public education system is nearing collapse."[10] Researcher Paul Hurd charges that "we are a generation of Americans that is scientifically and technologically illiterate."[11] Former director of the National Science Foundation John Slaughter warns of "a growing chasm between a small scientific and technological elite and a citizenry ill-informed, indeed uninformed, on issues with a scientific component."[12] Compounding an already critical problem is the fact that unqualified teachers are filling posts in critical subject areas. "According to the National Council of Supervisors of Mathematics, 26 percent of all math positions are filled by teachers uncertified to teach math."[13] In the crucial area of science, "the National Science Teachers Association estimate that as many as 40 percent of science classes across the nation are being taught by unqualified instructors."[14]

Why is it that the United States is falling way behind other industrialized nations in basic and yet vital areas such as math and science? Japanese students, for example, start specializing in math, physics, and biology in the sixth grade. Students in the Soviet Union start learning basic algebra and geometry in elementary school. Why is it that Japan, with a population half our size, graduates more engineers than we do? Why is it that the Soviets are producing almost five times as many engineers as the U.S.? Something is wrong!

We have discouraging results in other areas too. Note especially that the problem begins at the elementary level. U.S. Secretary of Education William Bennett reported in September 1986 that "91 percent of 13-year-olds were unable to write an adequate persuasive letter; 84 percent of 13-year-olds (and virtually all 9-year-olds) were unable to write an adequate imaginative essay; 81 percent of 18-year-olds (and 97 percent of 9-year-olds) couldn't produce a simple factual description requiring no opinion, creative thinking, or argumentation."[15] Similar elementary results have been discovered in math. Quoting a recent study by Harold Stevenson, Secretary Bennett noted that in mathematics the *highest*-scoring American fifth-grade classrooms failed to match even the *lowest*-scoring Japanese classrooms.[16]

The dismal academic performance among public school students can be attributed to at least five areas: 1) teacher incompetence, 2) textbooks, 3) grade inflation and automatic passage, 4) lack of discipline, and 5) teacher/parent/student apathy.

The area of teacher incompetence is a serious concern that has raised national attention. Though teachers have been getting more training in the past two decades than ever before, many are grossly deficient. Perhaps this explains why the average achievement of high school graduates has been steadily declining over the same period of time. Consider the following:

- An Oregon kindergarten teacher who had received A's and B's at Portland State University was recently found to be functionally illiterate.
- A third-grade teacher in Chicago wrote on the board:

"Put the following words in alfabetical order." Another Chicago teacher told a T.V. journalist, "I teaches English."

- A local school board in Wisconsin was outraged with teacher curriculum proposals which were riddled with bad grammar and spelling. Teachers misspelled common words: dabate for debate, documant for document, woud for would, seperate for separate.
- A fifth-grade Alabama teacher with a Master's degree sent a note home to parents which read in part, "Scott is dropping in his studies he acts as if he don't care. Scott want pass in his assignment at all, he a had a poem to learn and he fell to do it."[17]
- Houston teachers in 1983 shocked the school board when the results of a teacher competency test showed that 62 percent failed a standard reading skills test; 46 percent flunked in math, 26 percent in writing. But worst of all, of the 3,200 teachers who were tested, *it was discovered that 763 had cheated*.[18]

Under public pressure, many states are beginning to fight back with competency testing for teacher applicants. Recent polls show the teacher testing movement, while opposed by the N.E.A., is supported by 85 percent of U.S. adults. Those states that have enacted such legislation have uncovered skeletons they may wish had remained hidden from the public's eye. For example, in Louisiana, only 53 percent passed in 1978, 63 percent in 1979. The Pinellas County School Board in Clearwater, Florida, requires teacher candidates to read at a tenth-grade level and perform math at an eighth-grade level. About one-third flunked this testing requirement in 1979, even though all had their B.A. degree in hand. The same year, only half of the Mobile, Alabama, teacher applicants who took the National Teachers Examination (N.T.E.) passed it.[19] The incompetence of many public school teachers is a national disgrace. Is it any wonder so many American children are academically inferior?

I am not attempting to sound antiteacher, nor am I suggesting we go on witch hunts for the incompetents. That is not our objective here. I do think parents with children in school should be cognizant of growing teacher incompetence. It is important to expose those tools, methods, philosophies and even teachers which are potentially harmful to young minds. It must also be acknowledged, however, that there are still good teachers who are instructing their students in the best way they know how. Tim LaHaye has appropriately expressed this balanced and sober assessment of both kinds of teachers:

> Thousands of well-trained and very dedicated teachers still strive valiantly to give their charges the best education they can within a deficient educational system. Others, equally dedicated, were corrupted at our teachers colleges—with liberal humanist theories of education best described as "progressive education." Such brainwashed victims of our "high educational system"—a system controlled by secular humanists for over one hundred years—are really dangerous to the mental health of our children.[20]

School textbooks are also a primary target of academic concern, especially in four areas: lower standards, factual errors, ineffective methodology, and the stressing of nonessentials.

Concerning lower standards, former Secretary of Education Terrell Bell claims our textbooks had to be "dumbed down." That is, they had to be made less difficult because students could not handle the harder material.[21] Dr. Paul Copperman in his book *The Literacy Hoax* describes this in greater detail.

> Over the past ten years, most of the major textbook publishers have instituted a conscious policy of rewriting their textbooks in order to reduce their readability to a level two years below the grade for which they are intended. Thus, eleventh-grade American History books are being rewritten to a ninth-grade level, and twelfth-grade American Government texts are being rewritten to a tenth-grade level. This movement to reduce the readability levels of textbooks is widely known and accepted among secondary-school teachers and administrators, yet most parents have not been informed of it.[22]

What kind of commentary is this on public education? The old saying goes, "If you can't bring Mohammed to the mountain, then bring the mountain to Mohammed." This is apparently what American textbook publishers are doing. Instead of lowering our textbook levels, why not raise our student's intellectual capacities? The accommodation of student academic inabilities should simply not be tolerated.

Factual errors have been found in textbooks as well. Critiquers Mel and Norma Gabler report how they discovered fourteen errors on one page in a World Geography book. Significantly, eight of the errors favor Marxist countries and five of the other six errors are unfavorable to non-Marxist countries.[23]

A third area of textbook concern might be classified as ineffective methodology. One of the most striking failures in this area is the "look-say" method of reading instruction. That illiteracy is a national problem of crisis proportions has already been established. When you study the results of look-say methodology you will know why. The grossly ineffective look-say method used by 85 percent of our public elementary schools is believed to be the primary culprit of widespread reading problems and illiteracy. Extensive research by Dr. Jeanne Chall, a respected member of the International Reading Association and professor at the Harvard Graduate School of Education, and reading expert Dr. Rudolph Flesch has demonstrated that phonics is vastly superior to look-say methodology. This had been known for over thirty years when the late Dr. Flesch wrote his first eye-opening work, *Why Johnny Can't Read* (1955). In that book Dr. Flesch reported the results of 124 studies which all confirmed the superiority of phonics. Remarks Secretary of Education William Bennett:

> Most children are ready to read by First Grade and, when formal instruction begins, the teaching method is of great significance. From the 1920s until the early 1970s, a method called "Look Say" prevailed in American elementary schools; it relies on memorizing the meaning and appearances of entire words. But research of the past two decades has confirmed what experience and common sense tell us: that children learn to read more effectively when they first learn the relationship between letters and sounds. This is known as *phonics*.[29]

Look-say has never compared favorably with phonics.

Not surprisingly, as authorities like Drs. Chall and Flesch have spoken out against look-say, they have been quickly denounced by the publishers and promoters of such reading techniques. Moreover, look-say advocates quickly hire their own "experts" who attempt to divert attention from the overwhelming evidence by discrediting the look-say critics and rushing to assure the public that people like Flesch are twisting the facts. Other publishers have seemingly accepted the overwhelming evidence, only to alter their material into a quasi-phonics that still has the debilitating pull of "look-say" undercurrents.

But the crucial question is, why are 85 percent of our

public elementary schools still using the ineffective look-say method? On the other hand, why is Russia, whose literacy has been growing steadily, still using the phonics we discarded years ago? And why are most private schools still teaching phonics? Obviously, because it has much higher literacy results! Then why do the public schools persist in using the look-say method? Could it be part of an effort to undermine our nation's youth? One expert makes this astute observation:

> To believe that such massive functional illiteracy is an unplanned phenomenon beyond the control of anyone is to believe that our educators with all of their doctoral degrees literally don't know what they are doing. After all, teaching children to read is no big mystery. Teachers have been doing it for the last 3,000 years, and as the U.S. government's own statistics show they were doing it well in 1910 and up to about the 1930s when the big switch took place in teaching methods.[25]

Another method of teaching some consider dangerous is "mastery learning." This widely used method of instruction teaches children a specific skill or subject in small chunks. Thereupon, they are tested to see if they have mastered the skill. If they have not, they are retaught the skill using a different instructional method, and then tested again. This cycle can be repeated, supposedly, until mastery is achieved. Mastery learning can be applied to any subject area or skill.

Mastery learning was scuttled by the Chicago school system in 1985. A committee report to the Board of Education claimed the program's materials contained "grammatical errors, illogical instructions, reading passages too short for comprehension, disjointed units that provided little use of skills learned in actual reading, and test items that did not reflect what students were taught."[26] Further, Chicago parents complained that mastery learning denigrated parents, dealt with witchcraft and violence, and generally had a negative influence on their children.

A number of experts feel that mastery learning has a hidden agenda whose specific goal is to produce a uniform, predictable, and controlled citizenry. One research analyst states that mastery learning will teach children the bare minimum of traditional academic subjects while they learn how to be totally compliant, manageable robots.[27]

Charlotte T. Iserbyt, former official in the U.S. Department of Education, asserts that mastery learning is an international modification tool that will inculcate children with a whole new set of attitudes, values, and beliefs. In her recent book she states:

> So if your Johnny or Mary do (sic) not fit the internationalist social engineers' definition of "socially responsible," or do (sic) not have the "correct" pre-determined "character traits," they will be forced to "comply" through the use of behavior modification techniques. Of course, to the educationists, social engineers, and behavioral scientist, this is perfectly ethical since your children are nothing but human animals with no free will, souls, intellects or consciences. To the social engineers, they are the property of society, not the responsibility of the family. They are to be conditioned and trained like Pavlov's dogs, as was pointed out by Professor Allen Cohen, at a mastery learning conference he led in Maine, when he referred to our children at least four times as "human animals."[28]

The mastery learning method is already being used by some fifty million children around the globe. Benjamin Bloom, known as the father of mastery learning, has stated that he does not know of any major urban school system in America that has not adopted some kind of mastery learning program. Look-say and mastery learning are but two apparently ineffective methodologies used in our public schools.

Another dubious educational practice is "mentioning." Parental outcry that their children are not learning anything, combined with various state curriculum requirements, has led publishers to cram textbooks full of facts. Local school boards may then surmise that publishers are getting back to basics. Such endeavors, however, are sometimes done with little regard to literary style or meaning. As a result, points out analyst Harriet Tyson-Bernstein, textbooks get turned into "a dumping ground for facts"—not a tool for learning.[29]

The fourth area of textbook concern is the stressing of nonessentials. Let me cite two brief examples of this. First, a fifth-grade history book gave seven pages to Marilyn Monroe, while mentioning George Washington only eight times (and without telling about his accomplishments).[30] Secondly, one eighth-grade history text leaves out altogether crucial historical figures like Ethan Allen, Nathan Hale, John Paul Jones, David Farragut, and George Washington Carver. That same text, however, makes note of Bob Dylan, Janis Joplin, Gertrude Ederle,

Bobby Jones, Joan Baez, DuBois, and many others dear to liberal hearts.[31] Is Janis Joplin a more crucial historical figure than John Paul Jones? Dr. Max Rafferty, former dean of the School of Education at Troy State University asserts: "Until . . . a few years ago, most schools on all levels were teaching trivia. Today, tóo many—especially on the elementary level—are still doing so. If you doubt this, don't take my word for it. Visit classroom after classroom in widely separated regions of this country, as I have done."[32] It is unfortunate that we see the unnecessary exhibition of trivia and nonessentials in our classrooms and textbooks.

In these four areas (lower standards, factual errors, ineffective methodology, and the stressing of nonessentials) textbooks have slipped badly. This in turn has contributed to the overall academic decline of our students. Most parents do not want their children to be led astray or deceived by what is printed in their school textbooks. Do you? Evidently not only concerned parents feel this way, because in a nationwide poll of educators themselves, 93 percent suggested that curriculum materials need modification or should be scrapped altogether.[33] Ninety-three percent is not a slim majority—it is an overwhelming mandate.

The grave state of academic deficiency could also be attributed to grade inflation and automatic passage. Grade inflation is the deceiving technique of academic leniency which alters a student's grade upwards, making it appear that his ability is higher than what it really is. Experts have confirmed that students today get at least *25 percent more As and Bs* than they did fifteen years ago, but at the same time they *know less*.[34] After years of educational scrutiny, Dr. Paul Copperman observed that while courses were getting easier and reading and writing assignments were being reduced, high-school grades were moving upwards.[35] In other words, not only were class requirements getting easier, but so were grading standards. In a three-part series on educational shortcomings, the *Los Angeles Times* reported that "grades are threatening to become almost meaningless" due to teachers dropping traditional standards of academic quality and instead dispersing A and B marks offhandedly to a growing number of students.[36] Sooner or later, however, there comes a payday.

For example, *Newsweek* magazine featured a tragic consequence of grade inflation. A valedictorian of Western High School in Washington, D.C., was refused admission to George Washington University because of a low SAT score in both the math and verbal sections. Because his teachers were giving him excellent grades, he was deceived into thinking he was a real scholar. The unfortunate reality, however, was that he was not up to par with other acceptable collegiate applicants. The admissions dean at George Washington University exclaimed, "My feeling is that a kid like this has been conned; he's been deluded into thinking he's gotten an education."[37] The culprit of the con game? Grade inflation!

Grade inflation is a serious problem. In a study of high school students, Sanford Dornbusch polled a large number of metropolitan high school students about the grading methods of their teachers. About half felt that if they did poor work or did not try, they would still receive average or above-average grades.[38] What is this teaching our young people? It is teaching them mainly that "good work and hard work are almost pointless. Throughout their secondary schooling they learn that there is only a very tenuous relationship between effort and reward."[39]

Many conscientious educators are very concerned. "A survey of college professors revealed that 94 percent of the nation's college and university professors view grade inflation as a 'significant if not serious problem of academic standards,' and two thirds admit to granting higher grades than student work had warranted."[40]

What this can mean for parents with children in public school is this: your child's grades may not truly reflect his academic performance or skill. He may be the victim of grade inflation and might not be aware of it until after he receives the results of a standardized test. How disappointing for a high school senior to discover after his graduation that he had been strung along for years with a false sense of academic security.

Coupled with grade inflation is automatic passage—advancing students automatically from grade to grade no matter how deficient their academic performance. You need not look very far to find out how extensive the problem of automatic passage is. The shame of this practice comes when a graduate is hired based upon his completion of twelve grades, but then shows little of the skill and competency that should accompany a high school diploma. The victim of automatic passage will be in for rough sailing for the rest of his life.

A fourth area of academic failure can manifest itself when there is a lack of school discipline. A runner who competes for a prize is well acquainted with bodily discipline. He carefully watches his diet, ardently trains his leg muscles, and follows a rigorous exercise schedule. Without it, he would not have a chance at winning. Many youngsters today have little chance of winning in the academics race because of the lack of classroom discipline. More will be said on this subject later.

Finally, poor academic performance can result from teacher/parent/student apathy. If teachers do not care about their pupils or their academic growth, students will be hard pressed to gain ground in that subject. A Gallup poll revealed that teacher laziness and lack of interest are the most frequent accusations of half the nation's parents.[41] Students can permanently lose an interest in a particular academic field when a teacher does not care or when he poorly presents a certain area of study.

Parents likewise can be a negative influence on their child. One of the common complaints of teachers is parental apathy. Obviously, parents who are apathetic to their children's education should not consider home schooling. Dedication is a prerequisite for parents who want to home school.

Then there is student apathy, perhaps the biggest roadblock to academic achievement. Student apathy is often connected with the overall academic "environment" in the school itself. For example, when diligent students are ridiculed by their peers for doing their homework at night, many will buckle under the pressure, for they do not want to be labeled as an egghead. Slowly many begin to conform to academic lethargy. Unless a student's apathy is reversed, he will never aspire to be a success in life.

F in Morality

It is important to remember that when we speak of education, we are not exclusively referring to the intellect. A child also learns morality and value judgment, whether it is formally taught or not. A child is constantly in a state of learning. Many educational bureaucrats and antifamily proponents would have us believe that there is a neutral academic position. But who are they kidding? An academic learning environment is far from being neutral. A child who is publicly schooled will inevitably learn morality from both his teachers and his peers. The question is: What kind of morality is your child learning? And how is it affecting his character?

Consider what is happening to traditional family values in the public schools. Many Christian leaders feel that public school children are force-fed anti-Christian, antifamily points of view. Traditional marriage, the sanctity of a human life, love and respect for parents, and family integrity are often distorted or rejected. When this happens, public schools do not complement the family—they subvert it! If our public schools were teaching values in a positive light, then surely we would not have so much rebellion, sexual promiscuity, drug usage, delinquency, and violence among our nation's youth!

Dr. Paul C. Vitz in his recently completed study regarding religion and traditional values in public school textbooks concluded:

> When one looks at the total sample of 670 pieces in these basal readers the following findings stand out. Serious religious motivation is featured nowhere. References to Christianity or Judaism are uncommon and typically superficial. In particular, Protestantism is almost entirely excluded. At least for whites. Patriotism is close to nonexistent in the sample. Likewise, any appreciation of business success is essentially unrepresented. Traditional roles for both men and women receive virtually no support, while feminist portrayals regularly show women engaged in activities indistinguishable from those of men. Indeed, clear attacks on traditional sex roles, especially traditional concepts of manhood, were common.
>
> The above characteristics taken together make it clear that these basal readers are so written as to represent a systematic denial of the history, heritage, beliefs, and values of a very large segment of the American people.[42]

Testifying in a federal district classroom (Alabama, 1986) Professor Timothy L. Smith, a distinguished historian of American religion at Johns Hopkins, said he was "profoundly shocked" by the almost total lack of religious references in the state's eleventh-grade history texts. He pointed out that there was little mention of religion's role in the development of American pluralism or the "absolute central role" of Christians in the abolition of slavery.[43] In the same courtroom Dr. William Coulson, a professor of psychology at the United States International University in San Diego, criticized public schools for substituting psychology for hard moral reasoning. He cited a course on decision-making in family life in which never once "is it suggesting that [what is morally] right can be known."[44]

Consider the dramatic and far-reaching impact of the 1985

Supreme Court ruling on an Oklahoma state law. The Supreme Court decision restrains public schools from firing any teacher who advocates, promotes, or encourages public or private homosexuality in the classrooms. Bizarre, isn't it? Would it bother you if a homosexual teaches your child, perhaps even a sex education class, knowing that he/she can legally promote his/her lifestyle? It no longer matters what you think, for you have little choice in the matter. The Supreme Court ruling has widespread implications for public schools in every state.

A further 1985 Supreme Court ruling refused to allow Texas A & M University to ban a homosexual student group from campus. It appears that homosexual teachers and students have been permitted free reign in our public schools. Homosexuals, no matter how deviant and perverse one considers their lifestyle, can now teach children and "mingle" with them in the halls and classrooms. Will their teaching, influence, and presence promote traditional family values or be destructive to them?

Consider further some of the things being taught in public schools these days that instruct or infer a gutter morality: explicit sex education; texts which have lessons in violence, hate, and despair; values clarification; relativism; and death education. There are but a few specifics out of many that could be chosen. These six areas should suffice in illustrating the immorality that is often being taught in today's public classrooms.

Regarding *explicit sex education*, a father gave testimony before a U.S. Department of Education hearing in Seattle, Washington, in 1983, in which he described his son's fifth-grade health class. On the day he visited, he testified:

> A plastic model of female genitalia with a tampon insert was passed around to the boys so they might understand how tampons fit. Birth control pills were also passed around and explained. Anal intercourse was described. At no time was there any mention of abstinence as a desirable alternative for 5th graders. The morality that was taught in the classroom that day was complete promiscuity.[45]

In a similar hearing held in Concord, New Hampshire, on March 21, 1984 (seven such hearings were scheduled across the United States where hundreds of concerned parents, teachers, and citizens testified), another confused father testified:

> When my wife spoke to the school nurse about the health education program at school, the nurse told her that she delivers female students' urine samples to family planning clin-

ics for pregnancy testing. I never thought that schools work to educate therapeutically and test young girls for pregnancy. I always thought that schools had to do with developing learning skills and knowledge.[46]

These are not isolated examples, nor are they the worst. Much of what I have researched in this area is unprintable. It is not by accident that national surveys show that most Americans oppose teaching sex education without parental consent, while teachers favor it 61 percent to 36 percent.[47] Even their textbooks are saturated with it. Here are some actual examples taken from textbooks.

> Adolescent petting is an important opportunity to learn about sexual response and to gratify sexual and emotional desires without a more serious commitment.
>
> In many societies, premarital intercourse is expected and serves a useful role in the selection of a spouse. In such societies, there are seldom negative psychological consequences.[48]

One student health book had a caption underneath a picture of two young men embracing in a section titled "family health," which read: "Research shows that homosexuals can lead lives that are as full and healthy as those of heterosexuals."[49] Without a doubt, repeated sexual suggestions and fantasies in textbooks teach promiscuity, immorality, and homosexuality.

Homosexual men are the predominant patients and carriers of the decimating AIDS virus. The epidemic has erupted into an impending national catastrophe, and U.S. Surgeon General Everett Koop has offered the following as a solution:

> Education concerning AIDS must start at the lowest grade possible as part of any health and hygiene program. The appearance of AIDS could bring together diverse groups of parents and educators with opposing views on inclusion of sex education in the curricula. There is now no doubt that we need sex education in schools and that it must include information on heterosexual and homosexual relationships.[50]

There may be no doubt in the Surgeon General's mind, but there is extensive doubt in the minds of Christian parents all across America. Godly parents are infuriated at the suggestion that their children be exposed to ungodly sodomite activity, and especially when it is promulgated at the "lowest grade possible."

The Bible says, "It is shameful even to mention what the disobedient do in secret" (Eph. 5:12). To make matters worse, the Surgeon General further warns that "children with AIDS or ARC will be attending school along with others who carry the AIDS virus. Some children will develop brain disease which will produce changes in mental behavior."[51] Though we want to be compassionate to those who have acquired the dreaded disease, seriously and soberly ask yourself, "Do I want my child exposed to those inflicted with and suffering from the lethal AIDS contagion, some of whom will likely be manifesting signs of dementia (a state of brain deterioration resulting from the AIDS virus)?" In answering that question, keep in mind that this is perhaps the most devastating disease ever to ravage our population. There is no known cure in sight for this biological scourge; it is 100 percent fatal. Further, there remains considerable question and debate on some of the possible means of transmitting the deadly disease. Medical analysts simply need more time and facts to make absolute determinations about AIDS and its manner of transmission.

Another recent development affecting public schools is the travesty known as school-based clinics (SBCs). Since the first opened at Mechanics High School in St. Paul, Minnesota, in 1973, more than fifty have been established in high schools across America. Their function includes dispensing contraceptives, family planning, athletic physicals, laboratory and diagnostic screening, immunizations, nutrition and weight reduction programs, child care, and drug and alcohol abuse programs. However, though SBCs are being marketed as comprehensive health clinics, their main purpose appears to be the development of a contraceptive delivery mechanism into the schools. SBCs are being pushed by Planned Parenthood and other self-appointed advocates of teen sexual liberation who have consistently resisted efforts to require parental consent or notification for adolescent abortions and birth control counseling. Once a parent signs a "blank check" consent form for his son to receive a free sports physical, the SBC has the freedom to distribute contraceptives and engage in birth control counseling without parental notification or consent.

Statistics reveal that 62 percent of all females lose their virginity before the age of nineteen. Do SBCs help stem the tide of unwanted teen pregnancies through sex education and liberal contraceptive distribution as promoters intimate? To the contrary, they may have exacerbated the problem. A recent study of premaritally sexually active females aged fifteen to nineteen found that as sexual activity increases, the probability of pregnancy also increases—even when contraceptives are used consistently.[52] The House Select Committee on Children, Youth, and Families found that despite sex education and contraceptive distribution programs "there has been no change in the percentage of sexually active teens who become pregnant, but there has been a huge increase in the percentage of teens who are sexually active. And this increase in sexual activity has led to a proportionate increase in pregnancies to unmarried teens."[53] Even Planned Parenthood's own journal states that "more teenagers are using contraceptives and using them more consistently than ever before. Yet the number and rate of premarital pregnancies continues to rise."[54] Are SBCs worth the $25,000 to $400,000 per clinic it costs to operate them annually? Says SBC expert Barrett Mosbacker:

> In light of the fact that school-based clinics fail to reduce the pregnancy rate, will be involved in diagnosis rather than treatment, and offer services already available in most communities through private physicians and public agencies, such wasteful expenditures to initiate and sustain the school-based clinic program seem totally unjustifiable from a fiscal standpoint.[55]

Yet SBCs continue to grow in number each year, expanding their influence and their immorally suggestive activity.

Another moral disaster that has been unleashed in the public schools is drug availability and trafficking. Americans have consistently named drug use among the top problems confronting the nation's schools. Yet few realize how extensive and widespread the problem really is. A recent Department of Education report revealed that "The United States has the highest rate of teenage drug use of any industrialized nation. The drug problem in this country is 10 times greater than in Japan, for example. Sixty-one percent of high school seniors have used drugs."[56] But what makes the problem so heart-wrenching is where they are getting them—at school. A study of teenagers who contacted a cocaine hotline revealed that 57 percent of the respondents bought most of their drugs at school.[57] When the President of the United States intimates that our schools often resemble "drug dens" instead of "hallow halls of learning," we can safely assume we have a real problem on our hands. Despite stepped-up law enforcement activity, the problem continues to mushroom unrestrained. The percentage of students using drugs by the sixth grade has tripled over the last decade.[58]

Cocaine usage is the fastest growing drug problem in America. What makes it particularly alarming is its recent availability in a cheap but potent form called crack. Crack is a purified form of cocaine that is smoked. Here are some startling facts surrounding the mounting crack epidemic:

1. *Crack is inexpensive to try*—Crack is available for as little as $10. As a result, the drug is affordable to many new users, including high school and even elementary school students.

2. *Crack is easy to use*—It is sold in pieces resembling small white gravel or soap chips and is sometimes pressed into small pellets. Crack can be smoked in a pipe or put into a cigarette. Because the visible effects disappear within minutes after smoking, it can be used at almost anytime during the day.

3. *Crack is extremely addictive*—Crack is far more addictive than heroin or barbiturates. Because crack is smoke, it is quickly absorbed into the bloodstream. It produces a feeling of extreme euphoria, peaking within seconds. The desire to repeat this sensation can cause addiction within a few days.

4. *Crack leads to crime and severe psychological disorders*—Many youths, once addicted, have turned to stealing, prostitution, and drug dealing in order to support their habit. Continued use can produce violent behavior and psychotic states similar to schizophrenia.

5. *Crack is deadly*—Cocaine in any form can cause cardiac arrest and death by interrupting the brain's control over the heart and respiratory system.[59]

If your child is in a public school, he/she will not only be exposed to drugs, but will witness the illicit trafficking and casual usage of drugs. Powerful peer pressure will entice him/her to "fit in" or be socially ostracized. In the April 30, 1986, edition of the *Los Angeles Times*, California Attorney General John Van De Kamp stated, "It is a sad and sobering reality that trying drugs is no longer the exception among high school students. It is the norm."[60] Such environment is hardly conducive to moral stability and soundness of character.

A further problem, mentioned briefly above, is school texts which teach *violence, hate, and despair*. Perhaps this is one reason why every month some 282,800 persons are physically attacked in schools, 204 million high school students have something stolen from them, and six hundred million dollars are spent yearly on repairing vandalism.[61] Here is a violent poem found in a textbook used in many public schools.

Jack be nimble, Jack be quick
Snap the blade, and give it a flick
Grab the purse, it's easily done
Then just for kicks, just for fun
Plunge the knife, and cut and run. . . .[62]

How about this narration depicting a girl waiting to kill her brother:

She picked up a long knife which one of the boys had used to cut bread, and looked at its sharp-scraped edge. She would kill him. She sat straight in her chair, one hand resting on the table, the other holding the knife between her knees, concealing it in the folds of her nightgown. She kept her eyes steadily on the door, and Len came in. He started to walk around the table. "In a minute," she thought, "he'll pass me, and then his back will be turned. Then I'll kill him." Her fingers tighten on the handle of the knife.[63]

Many other school readers have been found to have graphic accounts of gang fights, raids by wild motorcyclists, violent demonstrations against authority, murders of family members, and rape.[64] Are these the kind of textbooks you want your child to read? Is it the kind of literature that impressionable young minds should read? Do your religious convictions allow you to accept such ungodly indoctrination? What responsible parent can condone the teaching of violence, hate, and despair?

There is also a technique called *values clarification*. This is a very subtle procedure that combines group sensitivity training and peer pressure. It rapidly exerts a very powerful hold on the moral development of young children. Dr. Tim LaHaye points out: "A much more accurate term for values clarification would be *morals modification*, because that is exactly what it is: the most poisonous technique ever devised for turning 43 million school children away from the traditional moral values of their parents and country."[65]

This evil technique is applied in a very controlled environment, where preselected concepts and questions are coupled with peer pressure and are usually far too advanced for those involved. It doesn't take long for the group to reprobate itself and arrive at debased conclusions when no moral absolutes are permitted in the discussion. This in turn creates in impressionable young minds an amoral attitude towards life. For example, imagine these actual textbook questions being debated where no moral absolutes apply:

- How many of you think there are times when cheating is justified?
- How many of you have ever had problems so bad you wished you could die so you wouldn't have to face them?
- How many would like to have different parents?
- How many would approve of a young couple trying out marriage by living together for six months before actually getting married?
- How many think a suspected homosexual should be allowed to teach in the public schools?
- How many think their parents should teach their children to masturbate?
- How many of you would choose to go to Heaven if it meant playing harps all day?[66]

Do questions like these have any place in the public classroom? Children go to school to learn usable skills, not how to question morality. The bottom line is this: whom do you want setting the values in your children, you or the school system?

A fourth area that undermines morality in our youth is *relativism*. Relativism is another dangerous practice which assumes that all values are situational. It teaches that the surrounding circumstances at any given time determine what is right and what is wrong. As we all know, situations are constantly in a state of change. Hence, the relativist teaches that what was "wrong" yesterday may very well be "right" today.

The term *situation ethics* was coined by a man named Joseph Fletcher. Fletcher, a professor at the Episcopal Theological Seminary, believed that Christian doctrine was "weird and utterly untenable" and so "de-Christianized" himself. His moral guide for judging all situations in life came to be based on its relevance to perceived human benefit.[67] In other words, moral decisions should not be based on the absolutes of God's Word, but on human feelings and judgments in any given situation.

An example of this becomes clear when we look at the wording in one sex education text. It says, "In a society where values are constantly shifting, the young adult may often be confused by which set of values he or she is to follow."[68] Really? This would lead a youngster to believe that there are no absolute morals which are applicable to every generation. Instead, it implies that each generation must develop its own values. Is this not antinomianism? Does it not create a feeling of "do whatever is right in your own eyes"? What parent wants his child subjected to such moral chaos?

A fifth area of moral concern in the public classroom comes from *death education*. As the name implies, this is the practice of exposing your youngster to death. Now that you are getting a feel for the content of many of our public textbooks, how many of these texts do you think present the Christian's firm belief in life after death? You guessed it!

One mother testified in a U.S. Department of Education hearing (Orlando, Florida, March 1984) that little first-graders were required to make their own coffins out of shoeboxes. In the same hearing, another mother testified that her daughter was given a list of ten ways to die, some of them violently. Her daughter was instructed to choose the most and least preferred. She was also asked what she wanted done to her if she was terminally ill. Two of the five preselected choices were mercy killing.[69]

One more example should suffice. You are looking at a picture of Jacqueline Kennedy and her daughter kneeling before the casket of assassinated President John F. Kennedy. Below it, your text instructs you to select an answer to a multiple-choice question, which has no right or wrong answers.

Is There Life After Death?
□ Strongly believe there is
□ Might be
□ Not sure
□ Probably not
□ Sure there is not[70]

Does this question present a solid moral conviction of life after death to your child? Or does it raise doubt in his mind that death ends it all? All death education tactics accomplish the same morbid goal of focusing attention on death and dying from a godless perspective. Do you want your child taught death from an anti-Christian perspective?

In each of these five areas—explicit sex education; lessons in violence, hate, and despair; values clarification; relativism; and death education—parents have good reason to be concerned about what their children are being taught. These are by no means an all-inclusive list of areas for moral concern. Many parents are completely unaware of what their child is being taught today in the public school. Do you really want to allow government-controlled schools this kind of power over your child?

F in Self-Image

Few things are as important to your child as his self-respect.* Indeed, developing a healthy self-image is the crying need among American youth today. Spiritual, mental, emotional, and physical upbringing all play an important part in your child's self-image. Effective learning requires self-respect. Lack of self-respect can stifle creativity, demolish leadership potential, and force will-less compliance and conformity to peer pressure. The question is: how are the public schools faring in the promotion of self-respect?

In his book *Self-esteem in the Classroom*, Verne Faust points out that "80 of every 100 so-called 'mentally retarded' children and adults are not mentally retarded. There's nothing organically deficient with their brains. Instead, they don't learn because of what happens to their self-esteem."[71] Amazing, isn't it? I wonder how many children and adults today are left with the impression that they are "slow learners" or "intellectually inferior" simply because of a lack of self-respect.

One of the primary sources of poor self-image may be the public school environment. Perhaps that is why student absenteeism is so high. If school were a positive environment, students would not be literally staying away from their classes by the millions, as they are. Why are some two and a half million enrolled students absent from their classes?[72] Why did a three and a half year study funded by the Carnegie Corporation find that "schools are oppressive and joyless"?[73]

If our schools are doing such a terrific job in building self-respect, then why is it that 50 percent or more of the nation's high school students report that they feel bored or negative about school? Why is it that half a million teenagers are so

---

*Throughout this book we will use the term *self-respect* instead of *self-esteem*. In many respects the two terms are synonymous. But since *self-esteem* has been used by the therapeutic community to refer to improper—even anti-Christian—kinds of self-love and *self-respect* has not, the latter term is preferable. Those quoted using self-esteem mean it in this proper sense of self-respect.

unhappy about themselves that they reduce painful anxiety through alcoholism? Why is it that one in five persons between ages thirteen and twenty-five is alcoholic?[74] Why is suicide the third leading cause of death among adolescents in the United States? Why is it that every year an estimated four hundred thousand young people between the ages of fifteen and twenty-four attempt suicide?[75] Why? Could a large part of the problem be because they have been robbed of self-respect by an uncaring educational system, insensitive teachers, and unbridled peer criticism? The schools certainly have the power to do so. Drs. Fantini and Young report that in many schools individual differences are neglected, conformity rewarded, and creativity stifled.[76]

Child psychologist Dr. James Dobson points out that there are two critical danger zones for your child's self-respect: physical attractiveness and intelligence. These are the two main "soft spots" where your child is most vulnerable.[77] These happen to be the two areas most exposed to ridicule and criticism in a public school environment. The world has both a heavy and unbalanced emphasis on beauty and brains, which often leaves children with severe scars in their self-respect. The key to overcoming these societal inequities is sensitivity. Children are extremely sensitive to critical comments about their height, weight, build, skin complexion, hair, or any noticeable flaw. They are also quick to absorb societal partiality toward intellectual brightness and are keenly aware of their "perceived" shortcomings.

Commenting on one way that self-respect is innocently assaulted in the classroom, Dr. Dobson gives this example:

> Miss Lodestar announces to her students that they are going to have an arithmetic contest. The ever-popular Johnny and Mary are asked to serve as captains, choosing team members alternately. Mary is granted first-draft choice and she grabs the ranking intellectual superstar, who moves to the side of the room nearest the captain. Johnny's first choice also goes to a kid with exceptional brain power. Through this entire process, dumb little Arnie is slumped down in his seat, knowing trouble is coming. He's thinking, "Somebody take me!" . . . The captains go on choosing until there's nobody left in the center of the room except Arnie, the local dummy. Johnny says, "You take him," and Mary says, "No! You take him!" Finally Miss Lodestar orders Johnny to include Arnie on his team. And sure

enough, when the contest begins, guess who flubs up? Guess who causes his team to lose? Guess who wishes he could curl up and die?[78]

Sound familiar? What if it had been a reading contest where children are particularly vulnerable? Either way, look what it did to that child's self-image. If your child is exceptionally bright, he might not encounter that problem. But there is still the physical area. Dr. Clyde Narramore, a well-known psychologist, describes being in a classroom where a teacher wanted to convey the concepts of "small" versus "large."

> She selected the tiniest little runt in the room, a withdrawn fellow who rarely made a sound, and instructed him to stand beside her at the front. "Small!" she said. "David is small." She then dismissed him and summoned the tallest girl in the class. "Large! Large! Sharon is very large!" said the teacher.[79]

What this humiliation before an entire class must do to a child's self-respect! We do not want to dismiss the parental contribution to low self-image, but neither should they get all the blame. One thing is for sure—public criticism before or by one's peers can be very damaging to self-respect.

Take time to evaluate your child's vital self-image. Is it basically positive and healthy? Or is it negative and low? Towards which are his school and peers contributing?

F in Discipline

Have you noticed what is happening in the area of discipline in our public schools? Twenty-five percent of parents in America fear for the safety of their child in schools.[80] A recent Gallup poll shows that the American public continues to regard discipline as the most important problem facing the public schools.[81] In fact, for fifteen out of the past sixteen years, the American public has ranked school discipline as the number one problem in education. It is not only parents who are concerned over a lack of discipline—teachers are worried as well. A survey taken by Metropolitan Life found that 95 percent of all teachers believe it would be a positive step to give much higher priority to school discipline and safety. Further, a 1983 poll by the National Education Association revealed that 28 percent of U.S. teachers had been victims of theft or vandalism and 4.2 percent had been attacked by students. Such misbehavior has had deleterious effects on teaching performance.[82] According to a National Education Association survey:

> Some 110,000 teachers—one out of every twenty—were physically attacked by students on school property during the 1978-79 school year. Another 10,000 were attacked by students off school property. The 110,000 victims represent an increase of 57 percent over the estimated 70,000 teachers who were attacked during 1977-78. Of the teachers who were attacked, an estimated 11,500 required medical attention for physical injuries and an estimated 9,000 required medical attention for emotional trauma.[83]

Another survey taken in 1985 shows the problem continues unabated. Some 640,000 teachers either had personal property stolen or intentionally damaged by a student within the twelve months previous to the survey, while approximately eighty thousand teachers were physically attacked by a student.[84] Perhaps this, in addition to low pay, explains why a 1986 Louis Harris poll reveals that 55 percent of classroom teachers have seriously considered leaving the profession.[85]

Also, students themselves suffer from senseless discipline problems. A survey by the National Association of Secondary School Principals found that middle school students listed the bullying and disruptive behavior of their classmates as their main concern.[86] How can a child learn under such appalling circumstances?

There is no excuse for allowing such blatant personal violence to continue. Schools should not be pens for undisciplined hoodlums, but hallowed halls of learning commanding respect for those in authority. Why then is it tolerated? Why are those who cannot appreciate the value of education not expelled or placed on work farms, so that children who want to learn have that opportunity? Why has discipline in our public schools been allowed to get so far out of hand? In describing his visit to Japanese classrooms, former U.S. Secretary of Education Terrel Bell pointed out:

> The Japanese educational system is superior to ours, if you measure quality by academic achievement in such areas as literacy and command of mathematics and science. *There is much more emphasis on order and discipline.*[87]

What has happened to discipline in our public schools? That is a very good question. Note, for example, the dramatic change in top offenses that have taken place between the 1940s and the 1980s in the public schools. In 1940 they were:

1) Talking
2) Chewing gum
3) Running in the halls
4) Wearing improper clothes
5) Making noise
6) Not putting paper in wastebaskets
7) Getting out of turn in line

As compared to the 1980's:

1)	Rape	11)	Absenteeism
2)	Robbery	12)	Vandalism
3)	Assault	13)	Murder
4)	Personal theft	14)	Extortion
5)	Burglary	15)	Gang warfare
6)	Drug abuse	16)	Pregnancies
7)	Arson	17)	Abortions
8)	Bombings	18)	Suicide
9)	Alcoholic abuse	19)	General disease
10)	Carrying of weapons	20)	Lying and cheating[88]

It seems evident to me that we have lost that essential quality of schoolroom discipline that we once had. And what about other treasured qualities like manners, common courtesies, etiquette, and personal grooming? Are they being encouraged or neglected in our schools? Some youngsters today have the social grace of a drunken sailor, the manners of a wild animal, the courtesy of a pompous fool, and the grooming habits of a pig. All these things fall in the area of self-discipline. Are they being fostered in your child's school? How important is it to you that your child develop these qualities?

Someone once asked Emily Post, an authority on etiquette, if manners are still important. She replied:

They are just as important to us now as they were to previous generations. . . . all good manners are based on thoughtfulness for others, and if everyone lived by the golden rule—"Do unto others as you would have others do unto you"—there would be no bad manners in the world. . . . A knowledge of etiquette—and good manners—carries many advantages. It imparts a comfortable feeling of security, self-confidence, and self-respect.[87]

How many schools work with parents in this vital area of personal development? How many care? One visit to your local school and you will quickly find out. Few people would dispute that good manners are the perfect complement to every facet of discipline.

If you are like most parents surveyed, proper school discipline is very important to you too. Some of you are probably frightened by what you see, but you do not know what you can do about it. Please, do not let anyone suggest that you must simply accept things as they are. That would be a compromise of your principles. If discipline is important to you, ask yourself, Is leaving my child with those who are unruly and undisciplined a hindrance or a help to his future?

F in Patriotism and the Promotion of Democratic Ideals

This is the final area in our imaginary report card, but a very essential one. You may ask, Surely our schools are not guilty in this area? Let's look at several examples, and then you decide. A mother and chairwoman for parent representatives in the Pittsburgh public schools testified before a U.S. Department of Education hearing in Pittsburgh, Pennsylvania, on March 16, 1984. In a portion of her testimony, she said:

> Plays presented to students with actors dancing on the United States flag are not uncommon and were a big problem here in Pittsburgh. Kids are definitely being programmed to accept a new global perspective.[90]

Would you want your child to witness such a disrespectful play in his school? Mel and Norma Gabler have uncovered numerous things very disconcerting in this area. State the Gablers, "The America of our forefathers is not beautiful in textbooks anymore. The welfare state, the United Nations, a hoped-for global world order, and communist revolutionary movements, are."[91] Does this not bring distress to your heart? They have further discovered that:

> Government subsidies and foreign aid are considered more effective than private enterprise, even though studies show the opposite more often is true. . . . The grandiose schemes of socialist third world governments are touted and their

failures hardly mentioned; governments allowing extensive freedom for free enterprise, if not given demerits, are ignored.

The most glowing paeans of praise are reserved for Marxist revolutionaries. How's this one for North Vietnamese leader Ho Chi Minh? "Ho Chi Minh was a man of action rather than one who created new ideas. For over fifty years, he fought for the cause he believed just. This fragile little man inspired genuine love among the people he led. He also won the grudging respect of his enemies." Left unstated are these facts: for decades Ho was a dedicated Communist. He eliminated other Vietnamese nationalist leaders through murder or by betraying them to the French. Ho's victories resulted in the death and imprisonment of millions. What textbooks leave unsaid often is more damaging than what they do say.[92]

Once again, there are many examples to choose from, but we will let this suffice. For those parents who want to investigate further what is in their child's public school textbooks, I encourage you to read Mel and Norma Gabler's book, *What Are They Teaching our Children?*

Is patriotism important to you? Do you want your child to grow to be a loyal American, faithful to his country? Are you tired of the assault on educational excellence? I believe that you are, or you wouldn't be reading this book. That is why it is essential to remove the blinders and see public education today as it really is. What is it really like? Dr. Tim LaHaye puts it very succinctly, "Secular educators no longer make learning their primary objective. Instead our public schools have become conduits to the minds of our youth, training them to be anti-God, anti-moral, anti-family, anti-free enterprise and anti-American."[93]

As a parent, you must decide if these are the things you want for your child, or if you want something better. The resolve of Christian parents all over this land is being tested and their convictions questioned. There are many (more than what you may think) who would like parents out of the education picture altogether. "The position is that the schools should be able to teach whatever they want to the schoolchildren—and that the schools should not be accountable to the parents for anything."[94]

A word about the NEA. The NEA was founded in Philadelphia in 1857. From the very beginning their goal was to create a national educational system, something our wise forefathers clearly left in the hands of state and local governments. At their very first organizational meeting, a call was made for a federal department of education. From that time forward it appears that they have been committed to the idea of government-owned and government-controlled schools.

Certain informed experts believe the NEA, with its carefully orchestrated and partially hidden agenda, has deliberately steered the public schools down the tragic road to socialism, humanism, radicalism, planned failure in literacy skills, suppression of Christianity, and the disposing of traditional values and beliefs. One thing is for certain—they are a tremendously potent political force, both locally and nationally, and their continual drive for more and greater power is both frightening and mind-boggling. The executive secretary of the NEA in 1967 predicted:

> NEA will become a political power second to no other special interest group. . . . NEA will organize this profession from top to bottom into logical operation units that can move swiftly and effectively and with power unmatched by any other organized group in the nation.[95]

Their activities have thus caused some observers to dub them the "educational mafia."

Now if the NEA is indeed a tool of the radical left, then their goals and purposes would be radically different than the teachers they represent. A recent poll (June 1985) of 1,007 randomly selected teachers found a wide disparity between the NEA and the rank-in-file members. For example, the NEA says teachers support busing. The poll, however, indicates that nearly 70 percent of its members oppose busing for the purpose of achieving racial balance.[96] Sally Reed, head of the National Council for Better Education, gives this description of the NEA:

> It has initiated policies which, in the end, have demoralized teachers, made their jobs more difficult, and compromised the legitimate needs of all educators.
>
> It has helped to undermine parental authority, and thus the family unit; it has portrayed itself as representative of teacher views when such is not the case.
>
> In short, the NEA has betrayed the public trust, and in the process created a negative attitude toward public school teachers and public education.[97]

The question is, why has the NEA been allowed to operate with impunity, considering its goals and excessive political activity? Why is this powerful teachers union, which is said to be secretly controlled by an elite board, even needed? However, since their members are firmly entrenched politically in all 435 congressional districts, state politics, and every school district in the country, how can concerned parents ever hope to win the war of what they teach your children? The resolve of the ungodly is strong and their purpose is clear. The January/February 1983 issue of *The Humanist* carried this battle cry:

> I am convinced that the battle for humankind's future must be waged and won in the public school classroom by teachers who correctly perceive their role as the proselytizers of a new faith: a religion of humanity that recognizes and respects the spark of what theologians call divinity in every human being. These teachers must embody the same selfless dedication as the most rabid fundamentalist preachers, for they will be ministers of another sort, utilizing a classroom instead of a pulpit to convey humanist values in whatever subject they teach, regardless of the educational level—preschool day care or large state university. The classroom must and will become an arena of conflict between the old and the new—the rotting corpse of Christianity, together with all its adjacent evils and misery, and the new faith of humanism. . . .[98]

There is no question about where they stand or what their goals are. To them it is all-out war, and your children are the booty. It is not a matter of "what" or "where"; to them it is a matter of "how soon?" This being the case, three all-important questions rise to be answered: One: how strong are your convictions about raising a godly, profamily, pro-American child? Two: are you willing to counter this radical anti-God movement with an equally radical commitment to your child's education? And three: are you ready to seriously explore your educational alternatives?

FOUR

Why Home Schooling Is The Best Alternative

Having examined the failures of the public school system, we now want to consider why home education is an excellent alternative. In light of the current performance of public education, responsible parents couldn't do any worse than the public school. Home schooling is one of several alternatives. A private or parochial school is certainly a better alternative than public education, but we want to demonstrate why home schooling, for those who are able, is also an excellent alternative.

Some might think home education is too radical, that all we really need to do is shore up the buckling public educational system. Change for the better, however, is unlikely for an educational structure with its own agenda and predetermined goals. Altering the status quo is probably the last thing the educational establishment wants. Hence, the late author/educator John Holt offers this experiential advice, "Don't waste your time and energy trying to change those institutions, think about taking your children out altogether and teaching them yourself, at home."[1]

Responsible and Loving Parents Qualify

One of the first thoughts of potential home schoolers is frequently, "I am not qualified." That is exactly what many educational bureaucrats want you to think. They do not want parents to even entertain the idea of teaching their own children. There are two commonly accepted reasons. First, parents who effectively home school expose the miserable failures and inadequacies of public education. Home schoolers are a growing threat to their educational monopoly. Secondly, home schoolers are seen as robbers of their vast enrollment coffers, since public schools receive funds according to their per capita attendance.

But loving and responsible moms and dads are qualified by virtue of their God-given responsibility and divine charge as parents (Deut. 4:9, 6:6-9; Prov. 22:6). God has not just made parents responsible; He has equipped them for the task. Many parents feel very unsure about themselves due to constant criticism. World health organization head John Bowlby has given this stern warning:

> The criticizing of parents and taking the children out of the home and putting them into the schools as is being commonly suggested these days actually undermines the parental confidence in the parent's own role, and in their potential role. There is entirely too much criticism. The educators are guilty of undermining the home rather than building it up.[2]

Bowlby has come to the conclusion that even a relatively bad home is generally better than a good institution. Except in the worst cases, he asserts, a mother "is giving him food and shelter, comforting him in distress, teaching him simple skills, and above all is providing him with that continuity of human care on which his sense of security rests."[3] Parents are capable of doing more than what they are given credit for. Despite what certain humanistic government officials say about them, parents are not just vehicles of procreation for the state. They are divine instruments of progenity whose parental purpose includes the overall development and oversight of their children.

At this point, it is essential that we define the word "qualified." It would be difficult to agree on who is or is not a good musician if we do not agree on what is or is not good music. Yet much educational propaganda tries to absolve teachers on similar grounds. How many educators agree on what makes a good teacher? Apparently not many, based on the dismal records of the school system. Further, when charged in court with negligence, educators defend themselves by saying that they cannot be judged guilty of not having done what should have been done because no one knows what should have been done. If this argument is accepted, then how can these same people who don't know what should have been done judge who is or is not competent to do it?[4] In the state of Texas it has been found that fully half of the teacher applicants scored lower in math than the average high-school junior, and a third scored lower in English. Personality ratings were deplorable. As former University of Chicago professor Don Erickson points out, a teaching certificate does not guarantee good teaching.[5]

Regarding the topic of teacher competence, John Holt says:

Educators . . . define "qualified" to mean teachers trained in schools in education and holding teaching certificates. They assume that to teach children involves a host of mysterious skills that can be learned only in schools of education and that are in fact taught there; that people who have this training teach much better than those who do not; and indeed that people who have not had this training are not competent to teach at all. None of these assumptions are true. . . .

As for the idea that certified teachers teach better than uncertified, or that uncertified teachers cannot teach at all, there is not a shred of evidence to support it, and a great deal against it. One indication is that our most selective, demanding, and successful private schools have among their teachers hardly any, if indeed any at all, who went to teacher training schools and got their degrees in education. Few such schools would even consider hiring a teacher who had only such training and such a degree. How does it happen that the richest and most powerful people in the country, the ones most able to choose what they want for their children, so regularly choose not to have them taught by trained and certified teachers? One might almost count it among the major benefits of being rich that you are able to avoid having your children taught by such teachers.[6]

For millennia parents have been passing along information and skills to their children. It is interesting that highly sophisticated societies have come from such "teaching methods." And throughout these many years there have been very few vocational teachers as we know them today. It has only been with relative recency that special training for teachers has arisen. People always knew that before you could teach something you had to know it yourself. But contemporary thinking espouses that before you can teach you must spend years being taught how to teach. This is not to say one should look pejoratively at teacher certification and educational degrees, but neither should parents be criticized and depreciated by haughty educrats who erroneously insist that they can do a superior job.

To be qualified as a Christian home educator, parents must

meet two requirements. First, they must be willing to develop, nurture, and exhibit a godly example. This means education begins with the parents and not with the children. Second, they must sit down and seriously count the costs involved before they make a decision to home school (Luke 14:28, 29). A deep interest and commitment to the home schooling process must be evident. They must be willing to make the time demands that home education will require. This may mean sacrificing certain unessential and superfluous activities that are often scheduled on life's agenda. If you meet these two basic requirements, you are indeed "qualified" to teach your own children. The requirements for being a good home school teacher are not unduly complex and do not require years of special training. "Parents need only be loving, responsive, and reasonably consistent, and salt these qualities with a little imagination, common sense, and willingness to follow a few simple suggestions."[7]

Without a doubt, the tutorial method of instruction is an excellent method of educational instruction. Home educators can emphasize total personality development in harmony (i.e., academic, moral, self-esteem, social, physical, spiritual). A child will become lopsided if one area is stressed to the detriment of another, or when one or several areas are left out altogether. All humans were meant to have their bodies and minds molded on a united front. We call this educating the whole man. In the atmosphere of a warm, loving home, much can be accomplished towards this end.

What I intend to demonstrate in this chapter is that home schooling, with the parental motivation of love, concern and sensitivity, can help children develop excellence in virtually every area of education. The five areas we will consider are academic, moral, social, physical, and spiritual.

Academic Superiority

It is hard for the public school officials to develop a sound case against home schoolers in academics because of their outstanding track record. Home schoolers are clearly superior when compared to many of their public school peers. Yet accusations are still made. Terry Herndon, while executive director of the National Education Association, charged that home schools "don't measure up to accepted standards," but the NEA has yet to produce one shred of evidence in support of this claim.[8] Let's consider some of the evidence.

A recent six-year Stanford study which compared home schooled children and traditionally schooled children found that home schoolers are significantly higher in achievement, behavior, and social perception. In a study of youngsters taken to court because of home education, the Hewitt Research Foundation has found that home schoolers achieve percentile scores 30 points higher than national averages on standardized tests. Over eighty studies comparing tutored children with those in a typical class have come to similar conclusions.[9]

Consider three specific instances where home schoolers have excelled in academics. The first involves five western New York state couples who taught their children at home and were challenged for truancy. Each family agreed to submit their children to the Stanford Achievement Test, one of America's most demanding measures. While the national average on this test is 50 percent, all seven children scored between 90 and 99 percent.[10]

The second instance took place in Wallace, Nebraska. A mother, with only a high school degree, began home schooling her daughter, who had been failing the sixth grade. Mrs. Rice began to teach her daughter about one to two hours a day, and then they worked side by side the remainder of the day in their family hotel. In nine months, her daughter's academic standing had risen almost three grade levels.[11]

The third example took place in Bonneville, California, where Mr. and Mrs. Colfax home educated their son Grant until he was eighteen. The parents were concerned about their boy's grasp of natural and physical sciences—subjects the parents knew little about. However, at age eighteen, Grant turned down a Yale offer and instead accepted a scholarship to study biology at Harvard. His fifteen-year-old brother, showing similar promise, has already constructed a twelve-inch refracting telescope.[12]

Most parents do not home school purely for academic reasons. But they could make a good case for it if they did. Responsible parents do not want illiterate, ill-informed children who perform poorly on major standardized tests. They want children who can read, write, and do arithmetic in a highly skilled manner. That is why so many have taken the satisfying step towards high academic performance by home educating their children.

Moral Excellence

Most parents who home school do so for a mixture of reasons. One of the most crucial on their list is the desire for moral excellence in their children. In 1981 Gunnar Gustavsen of Andrews University in Michigan surveyed 221 home school families. The most prevalent reasons given by these parents for withdrawing their children from public school were "concern for the *moral health and character development of their children*, rivalry and ridicule and violence in conventional schools, and the poor quality of public education."[13] Concerned parents do not want their child's heart and mind filled with moral sewage. Theodore Wade Jr., a professor of education at Weimar College in California, argues that parents are ultimately responsible for their children's moral values, no matter where they may be going to school. He further points out that public schools are necessarily "amoral" because they must serve families with conflicting moral values. Hence, Wade urges parents to assume the obligation to provide for their children's education themselves.[14]

Most home schooling parents aim for moral excellence. They know that morality is either "taught," "corrupted," or "ignored." Morality that is "taught" instructs and reinforces what is true, honorable, right, pure, honest, respectable, and good. The vast majority embrace godly values. Such parents believe that they, not the state, have the responsibility for the moral instruction of their children (cf. Eph. 6:1). Morality is "taught" when traditional attitudes, beliefs, and values are instilled with great care and determination. Home educators can successfully accomplish this using four means: 1) They carefully select the child's curriculum. 2) They instruct it orally. 3) They demonstrate it by personal example. And 4) They intertwine it with spiritual principles. A conventional school cannot accomplish this in a pluralistic system.

Morality is "corrupted" when it instructs and reinforces what is immoral, impure, unclean, selfish, sensuous, shameful—basically, those things which are unpleasing in the sight of God. It is conveyed by those who were themselves instructed with the idea that a good education must include knowledge of immorality. Usually their own lives have been polluted with a deeply-rooted humanistic philosophy. Such teachers do not always look the part. They may be young, polite, attractive, and nice and yet totally relativistic. These instructors have more potential for damage than those with more overt intentions. Who wants their children in the hands of either one? "Corrupted" morality pollutes the minds of young children, converting it into a cesspool for every kind of vile filth.

Morality is "ignored" when schools and teachers lead students to believe that morality has no absolutes. They teach whatever is vague and valueless, and that life is morally neutral. Proponents of this philosophy profess to be "amoral." But in reality there is no such thing. Morality is not "gray" or "borderline." It is either right or wrong, black or white, God-pleasing or not God-pleasing. When teachers attempt to instruct a class void of principles and values upon which students can make judgments, what are they really doing? They are creating a moral vacuum. And children left in a moral vacuum will absorb whatever prevailing values are at hand.

Christian home educators strive to "teach" morality, not "corrupt" or "ignore" it. *Webster's Dictionary* defines morality as "conformity to ideals of right human conduct."[15] But what is "right?" Rightness must be based on some set of values or principles. Traditional Christian morality is based upon the Bible. When children are so taught, they have a good chance of becoming morally sound and developing values which are solidly placed on the bedrock of God's abiding Word.

Further, home educators know the importance of instilling morality when children are young and their spirit and character are developing. If moral absolutes exist, as Scripture clearly states (cf. Romans 1), then to teach children moral relativism is un-Biblical and dangerous because it cannot distinguish between right and wrong. When morality is "taught" and embedded in young children, they are enabled to a much greater degree to deal with immorality later on. They learn how to resist temptation to do evil. They learn the significance of the word *no*, and can stand by it. Likewise, they also can say *yes* to those things which are pleasing in God's sight. With a strong set of values in their heart, their armor is solid and their fortification sound against immoral attacks. The Bible says, "Train a child in the way he should go, and when he is old he will not turn from it" (Prov. 22:6). What kind of morality do many children today give evidence of? Is it the kind you want for your child? Home schoolers strive for and usually achieve high moral standards in their children.

Healthy Self-image

Another area home schooled children can excel in is self-respect. This is one of the more important benefits of home education. A healthy self-image is a significant need among children everywhere. Self-respect is the capacity to see yourself as valuable and competent, loving and lovable, having certain unique talents and a worthwhile personality to share in relationships with others. It is definitely not conceited or self-centered, but demonstrates a realistic awareness of yourself and of your rights. In a sentence, it means to honor your uniqueness and, spiritually, to accept your life as a gift from God.[16] In a time when so many people lack this essential ingredient which builds strong character and good leaders, the home schooling movement is stimulating its revival.

Home schooled children tend to radiate a higher degree of self-respect and confidence because of three main factors: 1) absence of peer criticism and dependency, 2) parental nearness, and 3) parental monitoring and encouragement. Let's examine each one.

In a conventional school setting *peer criticism and ridicule* can play havoc with a young child's self-image. Children are often unknowingly brutal in what they say. Contrary to the juvenile saying, "Sticks and stones may break my bones, but words will never hurt me," words can do extensive damage to a young child's self-esteem. When placed in a setting where peer value assessments rule supreme, your child becomes subject to the societal judgments of worth. Dr. James Dobson correctly notes that society adjudicates your child's value on three factors: 1) beauty, 2) intelligence, and 3) wealth.

All it takes to be the target of criticism and ridicule at school is to have one perceived physical flaw, a seemingly slower learning ability, or to be poor. Imagine the emotional impact on a young child who has any one of these factors drawn to his attention. For example, one who is tall and slender is called "Lamp-post"; one that is short "Runt"; one that is redheaded "Carrot-top"; one that is heavyset "Porky, Fatso, Lard-bucket, or Tubby"; one that has protruding teeth "Buck tooth" or "Beaver"; and a hundred other names that go along with having freckles, large ears, heavy eyebrows, big nose, hairy arms, glasses, clumsiness, etc. And we all know that these remarks are mild compared to what is often hurled. Oftentimes criticism results not from actual but perceived flaws. Some names and comments are created out of sheer cruelty and meanness.

The same ridicule accompanies those who are slightly behind in intellectual development, for they are earmarked "idiot, stupid, moron, and empty-head." If one comes from a family in a lower economic bracket they ridicule their car, clothes, father's job, etc. Each remark, along with its accompanying body language and social stigma, has the crushing capacity to erode self-respect. It can alter the way children feel about themselves for years, perhaps for the rest of their life.

Two experts in the field of adolescent self-esteem write: "The way his peers perceive him strongly influences the adolescent's conception of himself, which generally remains unchanged throughout his life. Peer influences are at their zenith during preadolescence and adolescence when youngsters are most inclined to feel socially, emotionally, and even intellectually inept."[17] Child psychologist Dorothy C. Briggs points out that "no child can see himself directly, he only sees himself from the reflection of others. Their 'mirrors' literally mold his self image . . . what goes on between your youngster and those around him, consequently, is of central importance."[18]

In addition, the presence of peers in one's environment for seven hours a day, five days a week, often creates "peer dependency." Dr. Bronfenbrenner has found that a child who is peer-dependent loses a crucial sense of self-worth.[19] This is because he begins to trust the values and judgments of his peers more than his own or his family's. It is at this point that parents find it hard communicating and relating to their child, the so-called "generation gap."

One of the distinctive advantages of home schooling is the close control of destructive peer ridicule and criticism. In a warm home environment a young child is free to be creative instead of faddish, initiating instead of peer reliant, and individualistic instead of an age-mate cloned. At home school, peer criticism can be controlled or kept to a minimum. Children can be taught by the parents the importance of what Dr. Dobson calls a "no-knock" policy. They can be taught that constant self-criticism can become a bad habit and accomplishes nothing.[20]

A second reason home schooled children evidence self-respect is because of *parental nearness*. A child who grows up and is educated around a loving mom and dad will usually develop a good self-image. Maslow and Felker point out that a person with self-respect has a sense of "belonging."[21] Otto Weininger's studies confirm that children who remain home longer are more likely to demonstrate emotional "well-being."[22] John Bowlby says that numerous direct studies make it obvious that when deprived of maternal care, a child's development is almost always impaired physically, intellectually, and socially. Some children are gravely damaged for life. He further points out that "all" children under seven are vulnerable, and "many" who are much older than that.[23] Children place their highest value on parental nearness. The catalyst that develops and builds a child's self-respect is just being close and knowing the affection of Mom and Dad.

The third reason home schoolers shine with a good self-image is because it is carefully *monitored and encouraged*. Since parents are one of the primary architects of their child's self-respect, it is their primary responsibility to observe and encourage its growth. They can do this best when they home school simply because they are around their child the majority of the time. When a child receives a stinging remark from a neighborhood playmate, Mom and Dad can help them counteract it and deal with the pain. When they can't grasp an area of schoolwork and feel incompetent, Mom and Dad can give them immediate comfort and reassurance of their abilities. Parents are not to eliminate every challenge for their children, but just serve as a confident ally in their behalf, encouraging when they are distressed, intervening when the threats are overwhelming, and above all, giving them the tools to overcome the obstacles.[24]

Regarding your child's self-respect, no one has summed it up more distinctly than developmental psychologist Dr. James Dobson. He says:

> The building of self-esteem in your child is one responsibility which cannot be delegated to others. The task is too difficult and too personal to be handled in group situations. Without your commitment and support, Junior is on his own against formidable foes. With few exceptions, our materialistic society is not going to reinforce healthy self-concepts in your children, and if these desirable attitudes are to be constructed—only you can do it. No one else will care enough to make the necessary investment.[25]

How important is self-respect? It is apparently the foundation of every sound quality desirable in human beings. George Gallup Jr. recently conducted a poll on the self-respect of the American public. The poll conclusively showed that people with a strong self-image demonstrated the following qualities:

1. They have a high moral and ethical sensitivity.

2. They have a strong sense of family.

3. They are far more successful in interpersonal relationships.

4. Their perspective of success is viewed in terms of interpersonal relationships, not in crass materialistic terms.

5. They're far more productive on the job.

6. They are far lower in incidents of chemical addictions.

7. They are more likely to get involved in social and political activities in their communities.

8. They are far more generous to charitable institutions and give far more generously to relief causes.[26]

Are these not the qualities that you want your child to have? If so, then the building of self-respect in a culture where so few have it becomes paramount. A tactical approach must be seriously considered. How are you going to build and develop it in your child? One thing is for sure; by lovingly and responsibly home educating your child, you can help him build and develop a healthy and positive self-image.

Socially Well-adjusted

Another bright spot for home schoolers is their sociability. However, socialization is also a key area where home educators are often unjustly criticized. Frequently those who do the criticizing have bought into a common but false notion. In reality, home schoolers are some of the best socially-adjusted people around.

Perhaps the place to begin here is with the word *socialization*. There are two types of socialization: positive and negative. Positive socialization helps a child to grow and develop to his full potential in life. When a child's personality develops in a warm atmosphere of love and acceptance, he will usually socialize well with all age groups, including his own. Negative socialization, on the other hand, separates a child from his parents and restricts a child's socializing primarily to his age-mates. This can have detrimental and long-term affects on a child's potential sociability among a wide age dispersement.

It is precisely because they spend most of their time around Mom and Dad that home schooled children are able to engage socially in multi-age situations with a high level of confidence. Home educated children to a large degree adopt the values and sociability of their parents. On the other hand, studies have shown that a child placed into an institutional setting before he has an understanding of his own values will lock into the value systems of his age-mates. Because he spends more time with his peers than with his family, he becomes peer-dependent, adopting the habits, mannerisms, and language of those around him.[27] The May/June 1986 issue of *The Parent Educator and Family Report* gave this summary of research results performed by Dr. John Wesley Taylor of Andrews University.

> Based on one of the best-validated self-concept scales available, a random sampling of home school children from approximately 45,000 home schooling addresses found that half of these children scored "at or above the ninety-first percentile"—41 percent higher than the average, conventionally schooled child. Only 10.3 percent scores below the national average. Since self-concept is considered to be a basic dynamic of positive sociability, this answers the often-heard skepticism suggesting that home schoolers are inferior in socialization.[28]

Some educators argue that home school parents are protecting their children from the "real world." Most home schoolers would probably disagree. What is the real world? It may be begging the question, but we do well to address the following: is the real world that lifestyle embellished on T.V. and movie screens with their sordid wickedness and vile filth? Is the real world primarily made up of violence, crime, rebellion, fornication, murder, perversion, and greed? Many would like your child to think so. Is this the true makeup of the real world? Or is the real world that which emanates from and is dependent upon almighty God; that which is good, honest, principled, and true? Is not the real world under the control and auspices of the living God?

Further, some contend that the "realities" which children need exposure to consist of dirty language, rebelliousness, and a vile, degenerate environment. They argue that since this is what life is "really" like, children need to be "exposed." But this is an unsatisfactory argument that most home educators simply aren't buying. It is true that there is a measure of sheltering that exists among home schoolers. But is this not the place and function of the home? Responsible, godly parents should stand as a buffer between their tender, young child and the evil harshness of his world. Parents should not allow their children exposure to the raw onslaughts of worldliness and demonic activity, all in the name of "socialization." Nurseries grow seedlings in greenhouses, because that is where they grow best. The new plants can flourish because they are protected from subfreezing temperatures and strong winter winds. When spring arrives, the plants are stronger and more mature and ready to be transplanted. Soon they are ready to become productive. But the early sheltering was a necessary part of the growth process. Children too need time to grow and be trained in the Word of God before they are ready for the stark realities of the world. Protection and godly training in the early years make a child stronger and better prepared for the world—not weak and unprepared, as some suggest. As a result of a certain amount of sheltering, they can become productive citizens, bearing the fruits of the godly life in Christ Jesus.

Parents should not feel obligated in the least to subject their children to a hedonistic and debauched philosophy of life for the sake of exposure. That line of reasoning is totally without merit. It naturally leads into the idea that if a little exposure is good, then more exposure is better. The implications from here are obvious.

The fallacies of the socialization argument come to light when they are put under careful scrutiny. When a child is young, not even a little exposure to evil is proper. Who wants a little exposure to the AIDS virus just to know what it is like? No one! Exposure for the sake of exposure is a bankrupt argument. Those who buy it will pay a high price.

The pages of Scripture are replete with examples of this. Righteous Lot tried living among the evil men in the city of Sodom. Though he loved God, the city's powerful influence overwhelmed his family's convictions, leading to his wife's death and corrupting the morals of his daughters (Gen. 18:22—19:38). Because he was peer dependent, young King Rehoboam ignored the counsel of his elders, and instead tragically followed the advice of the boys he grew up with (cf. 1 Kings 12:1-6). We may think our child is strong enough to ignore or stand up against negative socialization, but the Bible clearly states that "bad company corrupts good character" (1 Cor. 15:33). Like Joseph, sometimes the best thing we can do for our child is to help him flee that environment that so easily sways him away from God (cf. Gen. 39:7-12). This refutes the argument that Christian children need to stay in public school to be a witness. Biblical history makes clear who is most likely to be influenced, especially at that age. Only when evil is seen in the light of God's displeasure and His just retribution does it benefit a child.

Once we clear away the semantic underbrush, we can decide intelligently what kind of socialization we want for our children, positive or negative. As has been pointed out, home schooled children engage in the former. The results demonstrate that home educated children are indeed socially well-adjusted, often in a superior way to those who are conventionally schooled.

Physical Stamina

There is no magic here. Home schoolers have more physical stamina because parents can easily monitor their diet. Recently I talked with a public school teacher who said it is not uncommon for students to have a Coke and potato chips for lunch. What kind of nutrition is that? Why is it that "13 of every 100 elementary school children are obese. And as many as 40 percent of all youngsters suffer obesity."[29] It is conceded that some obesity problems are due to metabolism and chemical imbalance, but the vast majority are due to diet. Most nutritionists agree that colas, chips, candy, sweets, and carbohydrates consumed in large quantities can adversely affect a child both physically and mentally.

Home schooled children can be monitored carefully to insure ingestion of wholesome, nutritious, vitamin-packed meals. Tests have been performed that show a definite correlation between diet and mental acuity. These same tests show diet also can affect one's personality.[30] It naturally follows that responsible parents will want to control their children's diet and maximize their learning ability. Home educators can do this better than anyone else.

In addition, they can encourage and oversee a systematic exercise program. The first national conference on youth fitness, held in 1984, discovered that fewer than 50 percent of children in the six to seventeen age bracket meet desirable fitness levels. Home educators can offer their children a wide variety of physical exercise through community recreation centers, local sports, and family-centered activities. Physical education is often more pleasurable to home schooled students because they are not confined to the track field and gym, and because they do not have to endure the competitive atmosphere of a school locker room. Public showers combined with peer ridicule have probably done more to damage an adolescent's body image than anything else. Home schoolers avoid such emotionally dangerous situations, which can affect a child's enjoyment of physical education.

Finally, because home schooled children do not have to sit behind a desk so long, they can enjoy a greater amount of recreation throughout the day. The physical argument alone is not the strongest reason for home schooling, but it is one which when combined with other factors makes home schooling a distinct advantage.

Spiritual Depth and Appreciation

All areas considered, this is the one where home schoolers can shine the most. It is true that most who home school do so because of religious convictions. This is also what gives home schoolers their power and effectiveness. Hence, most of them utilize their educational opportunity to promote spiritual depth and appreciation.

We want to look at five areas of importance in this matter of spiritual development: 1) the priority of spiritual teaching, 2) where public schools and the state stand on this issue, 3) what the Bible says about the parental role, 4) religious conviction vs. religious preference, and 5) the home schooling advantage.

The most important area of education and training that parents are charged with giving their children is spiritual. This is to be the *number one priority*. Everything else should take second seat to this. When a young mind and heart is stripped of divine guidance, direction, and help, the results are catastrophic. To avoid such a catastrophe, where does an educator start in his instruction of a child? How does a child become wise? The Bible clearly acknowledges that "the fear of the Lord is the beginning of wisdom" (Proverbs 9:10). And this "fear of the Lord" only comes when priority is placed on the teaching of the Word of God. Back in the sixteenth century the great reformer Martin Luther made this astute prediction:

> I am much afraid that schools will prove to be the great gates of Hell unless they diligently labor in explaining the holy scriptures, engraving them in the hearts of youth.
>
> I advise no one to place his child where the scriptures do not reign paramount. Every institution in which men are not increasingly occupied with the word of God must become corrupt.[31]

Martin Luther wisely foresaw the danger of Biblical erosion in educational circles. Such an atmosphere leads to an assumed spiritual self-sufficiency, which plants the seeds of godlessness, rebellion, and immorality. If parents are to take seriously Martin Luther's advice, their primary educational concern should be: "Is my child diligently being taught the Word of God? Are Scriptural seeds being planted in his heart, being fed and watered, nurtured and helped to grow?" The Bible says, "See to it that no one carries you off as spoil or makes you yourselves captive by his so-called philosophy and intellectualism, and vain deceit (idle fancies and plain nonsense), following human tradition—men's ideas of the material [rather than the spiritual] world—just crude notions following the rudimentary and elemental teachings of the universe, and disregarding [the teachings of] Christ, the Messiah . . . let the word [spoken by] the Christ, the Messiah, have its home (in your hearts and minds) and dwell in [all its] richness" (Col. 2:8; 3:16, *Amplified Bible*).

This leads us to our next point, *Where do public schools and the state stand on this issue*? The following examples illustrate some of the extremes which certain school districts are engaging in. Many schools have stopped scheduling spring break around Easter to avoid the appearance of advancing religion. And in Kanawha County, West Virginia, school officials ordered all Bibles to be removed from school premises and dumped in an incinerator.[32] Not every school system has taken steps this radical, but the fact that these things have even happened in America show the degree of ideological transition that has taken place. Many more schools operate with more subtle means.

Consider further the direction of the Supreme Court in the past thirty years. In 1954, in *Gideons International v. Tudor*, the Supreme Court let stand a New Jersey law that declared Bible distribution in public schools unconstitutional. The Gideons, as you are probably aware, have a long history of providing free Bibles to students, servicemen, prisoners, nurses, etc. In 1962, in *Engel v. Vitale*, the Court held unconstitutional nonsectarian school prayer. One year later came the landmark decision of *Schempp/Murray*, which was a catastrophic setback for Christianity in America. This 8-1 Supreme Court decision declared devotional reading of the Bible and school-sponsored prayer (in this case, the Lord's Prayer) unconstitutional. Madalyn Murray O'Hair and her cohorts won a major victory for national atheism and the humanizing of public schools. To further demonstrate the Court's tenacious drive to root out every hint of Christian influence, we merely look at *Netcong*. This 1971 decision ruled that prayer reading in school before formal opening of classes violated the First Amendment, even though (in this case) the *prayers were taken from the Congressional Record* and *attendance was voluntary*. Incredible, isn't it? This is shocking in light of the fact that the majority of the American public wants it back. A recent Gallup poll shows that Americans approve of voluntary school prayer by a 4-1 margin.[33] Nevertheless, current law considers it unconstitutional.

Individual states began to respond to this ludicrous shift in public educational policy. The State of Kentucky, wanting to keep at least a hairsbreadth of moral direction in the schools, passed a law that required the posting of the Ten Commandments in public school classrooms. But in 1980 the Supreme Court struck again and declared the Kentucky law unconstitutional. This clearly reveals the Supreme Court's untiring attempts to repudiate the Biblical basis of American society. How can your child grow spiritually in an educational system that has been Biblically and morally neutered by the Supreme Court?

Thirdly, let's consider the *Biblical view of parental responsibility in the matter of spiritual training*. Below is a review of relevant Scriptures that highlight parental duty:

Deuteronomy 4:9—Only be careful, and watch yourselves closely so that you do not forget the things your eyes have seen or let them slip from your heart as long as you live. Teach them to your children and to their children after them.

Deuteronomy 6:1, 2, 6, 7—These are the commandments, decrees and laws the Lord your God directed me to teach you to observe in the land you are crossing the Jordan to possess, so that you, your children and their children after them may fear the Lord as long as you live by keeping all his decrees and commands that I give you, and so you may enjoy long life. . . . These commandments that I give you today are to be upon your hearts. Impress them on your children. Talk about them when you sit at home and when you walk along the road and when you lie down and when you get up.

Deuteronomy 11:18, 19—Fix these words of mine in your hearts and minds; tie them as symbols on your hands and bind them on your foreheads. Teach them to your children, talking about them when you sit at home and when you walk along the road, and when you lie down and when you get up.

1 Samuel 1:28; 2:26—"So now I (Hannah) give him to the Lord. For his whole life he will be given over to the Lord." . . . And the boy Samuel continued to grow in stature and in favor with the Lord and with men.

Psalm 78:1-7—O my people, hear my teaching; listen to the words of my mouth. I will open my mouth in parables, I will utter things hidden from of old—things we have heard and known, things our fathers have told us. We will not hide them from their children; we will tell the next generation the praiseworthy deeds of the Lord, his power, and the wonders he has done. He decreed statutes for Jacob and established the law in Israel, which he commanded our forefathers to teach their children, so the next generation would know them, even the children yet to be born, and they in turn would tell their children. Then they would put their trust in God and would not forget his deeds but would keep his commands.

Proverbs 4:3-5—When I was a boy in my father's house, still tender, and an only child of my mother, he taught me and said, "Lay hold of my words with all your heart; keep my commands and you will live. Get wisdom, get understanding; do not forget my words or swerve from them."

Proverbs 22:6—Train a child in the way he should go, and when he is old he will not turn from it.

Galatians 4:2—He (a child) is subject to guardians and trustees until the time set by his father.

Ephesians 6:1-4—Children, obey your parents in the Lord, for this is right. "Honor your father and mother"—which is the first commandment with a promise—"that it may go well with you and that you may enjoy long life on the earth." Fathers, do not exasperate your children; instead, bring them up in the training and instruction of the Lord.

1 Thessalonians 2:11, 12—We dealt with each of you as a father deals with his own children, encouraging, comforting and urging you to live lives worthy of God, who calls you into his kingdom and glory.

Many other Scriptures teach by inference the same thing. The Apostle Paul commended Timothy's mother and grandmother who "from infancy" taught him the "holy Scriptures" (2 Tim. 3:15). The local pastor/overseer was to meet certain qualifications, which were to serve as a model to other fathers in the church. Two of these qualifications stipulated that he was "able to teach" and "to manage his own family well and see that his children obey him with proper respect" (1 Tim. 3:2, 4). Young mothers were called on to "love their children" and be "busy at home" (Titus 2:4, 5).

In addition, numerous other Scriptures exhort on the purpose, power, and needed preeminence of the Word of God in the lives of people. Here are three of them:

Matthew 7:24-27—"Therefore everyone who hears these words of mine and puts them into practice is like a wise man who built his house upon the rock. The rain came down, the streams rose, and the winds blew and beat against that house; yet it did not fall, because it had its foundation on the rock. But everyone who hears these words of mine and does not put them into practice is like a foolish man who built his house on the sand. The rain came down, the streams rose, and the winds blew, and beat against that house, and it fell with a great crash."

2 Timothy 3:16, 17—All Scripture is God-breathed and is useful for teaching, rebuking, correcting, and training in righteousness, so that the man of God may be thoroughly equipped for every good work.

1 Peter 1:24, 25—"All men are like grass, and all their glory is like the flowers of the field; the grass withers and the flowers fall, but the word of the Lord stands forever. . . ."

How can parents omit or be negligent in teaching their children the Word of God? By delegating the crucial task to others without proper parental participation, oversight, and accountability. This is one job that is far too important to just leave to others! In God's eyes, parents are ultimately held accountable for the job and how well it is administered.

The fourth area we want to consider is *religious conviction versus religious preference*. This is quite important! If you should choose to home school your child on religious grounds, you should at least understand the difference between these two.

When you home educate on religious grounds, it is legally the most defensible when it is based on a conviction. Succinctly stated, a religious preference is a simple desire or want, but a conviction implies that one has a fundamental, compelling interest. The U.S. Supreme Court, in the *Yoder v. Wisconsin* case, mandated that the free exercise of religious convictions may not be abridged by any law or state. In that 1972 case, a compulsory education statue was challenged by the Amish, because they chose vocational home education in the years after grade eight through age sixteen. The Court ruled in favor of the Amish, stating that they were "protected by the free exercise clause of the First Amendment, and the *traditional interest of parents with respect to the religious upbringing of their children . . .*"[34] (emphasis mine).

Those who choose to home school as a result of strong religious conviction instead of just as a preference will find their position the most legally defensible. In addition, they will find that home schooling will take on a new meaning, one of deep-rooted parental interest and concern.

Finally, we want to consider why *home schoolers have an advantage in building spiritual depth and appreciation*. There are three reasons. First, you can select what your child is being taught spiritually. If your child is in a conventional parochial school, he will be taught the doctrines of the church which sponsors that school. If you are not affiliated with that denomination, you must settle for whatever they teach. Home educators can tailor their spiritual instruction to conform to their beliefs and convictions.

In addition, home educators have a spiritual advantage when it comes to building character. When parents identify an area of character weakness in their child (e.g., lack of patience, trust, joy, forgiveness), they can immediately begin to stress the character trait that fills the child's need. Most parochial schools would find it very difficult to individualize their character training. As a result, they lose a sensitivity to minor character flaws which can mushroom in later life.

Lastly, home educators have an advantage in this area because spiritual growth to a much greater degree becomes a family experience. Children learn primarily by example, emulating the spiritual model of those around them. If they are with their peers, they will emulate them; if with parents, they will emulate them. When a child can read the Bible with Mom and Dad, pray together, share joys, and deal with problems together, this creates a unique spiritual bonding that is dynamic and inexplicable. Best of all, it creates a spiritual depth and appreciation second to none.

When all is said, home schooling that is lovingly and responsibly carried out has a superior report card. In the areas of academics, morality, self-image, social adjustment, physical care, and spiritual growth, home schooling has a terrific track record. Home schooling is an excellent educational alternative and may very well be the best for you.

Advantages of Home Education as a Tutorial Method

Tutorial (one-on-one) education offers many special teaching advantages. Perhaps this explains why the children of royalty have always been educated by this method. Responsible Christian parents can make excellent tutors. There are eight teaching advantages afforded to those who home tutor over against all other educational alternatives.

1) *Home educators do not have to contend with the disadvantage of large classes.* In most conventional schools, teachers have to contend with twenty, thirty, or more students under varying circumstances, leaving little time for one-on-one personal encounters. Despite a good teacher's best efforts, this can often impede the learning process. Home educators, on the other hand, are able to engage in relatively large amounts of one-on-one instruction. This enables them to provide a quality education, and with far less time and expense.

2) *Home schooled children avoid the dangerous peer pressure that of necessity still exists in community-style education.* Large classroom instruction has never been proven to be a superior method of teaching, but is used in order to accomplish the goals of mass education. Researchers have found that the tutorial method of instruction has never been excelled by institutions when it comes to fundamental learning.[35] One unfortunate result of community-style education is peer pressure. Wherever there are peers, there will be an inheritance of peer pressure. The more peers to contend with, the greater the stress of such pressure. The younger the child, the more harmful its effects. Worst of all, peer pressure unknowingly often produces peer-dependency, a regrettable and time-revealing flaw of such instructional methodology. Peer-dependent children have a negative view of themselves. They also show much greater concern for what their peers think and say than what their parents think and say. Extensive child development research has found that peer-dependent children "are pessimistic about the future, rate lower in responsibility and leadership and are more likely to engage in such anti-

social behavior as lying, teasing other children, playing hooky or doing something illegal. . . . More serious manifestations are reflected in the rising of youthful runaways, school dropouts, drug abuse, suicide, delinquency, vandalism and violence documented for the White House Conference of Children in 1970."[36]

The pressure placed on a child by his peers can be awesome. Such pressure will eventually affect the parents. For example, how many parents ended up buying their daughters a Cabbage Patch doll simply because it was the thing to have? The Cabbage Patch craze swept our nation's children like wildfire and made its inventor a multimillionaire. But it also left its impact on parents and their pocketbooks. There are, of course, many other ever-changing fads children can succumb to. The fad may not be evil per se, but it indicates the persuasiveness of peer pressure and also how the media manipulates weakness in this area. How much more dangerous is such peer pressure when it involves moral issues. The tutorial method of instruction can circumvent these potentially damaging age-mate pressures.

3) *Home schoolers develop a unique bond of closeness with their parents*. This unique bonding has the potential for producing deeper interrelationships, love, trust, and family dependency. This in turn produces more meaningful communication, emotional intimacy, and a closer family life. In a day when teen-age/parent communications are often shallow and inadequate, home schooling offers you time with your child—time to talk, time to build relationships, time to interact, time to share frustrations and joys, and time to mold Christian attributes.

One home schooling mother, who took her two daughters out of a conventional school, commented on how they are *redeveloping* love and affection for each other. She said, "They used to get along so well until they started school. Before long they began to fight and bicker with one another. Since we started home schooling, they are once again learning to love and get along with each other. There is less rivalry and strife." Hence, this unique bond of closeness extends not only to parents, but also to brothers and sisters.

4) *Home schoolers can enjoy their children more*. It follows quite naturally that when you are around the ones you love the most and vice versa, you get great enjoyment out of it. I can think of no greater pleasure for a parent than to watch his child grow, develop, and share his life's experiences. If there is any tragedy of modern family life today, it is the fact that parents

don't enjoy their children as much as they could. One of the most common parental regrets I have heard over the years in the counseling room is that they didn't spend enough quality time with their children while they were growing up. They wish they could turn back the hands of Father Time. But as we all know, that's impossible. Conventional schooling leaves you potential time with your child in the evenings and on weekends. I say "potential," because by the time you subtract personal time, eating and hygienic necessities, playing, recreation, homework, extracurricular school activities, dating, etc., how much time is left for enjoying your child? Home schooling will not solve every time obstacle, but it will give you more time to enjoy your child.

5) *Home schooled children can avoid the unhealthy atmosphere of early education*. Many development psychologists have attested to the inherent dangers of early education. Here is how Dr. Moore puts it:

> For most children, reasonable maturity for formal learning seems to bring together or integrate all their senses and organs between the ages of eight and ten or eleven. We call this chronological age period the *integrated maturity level* or the optimum time for most normal children to start school, entering at the level of their age-mates at grade three, four, or five. They will quickly catch up and usually pass the children who started earlier. Parents can judge the maturity of their children within the eight-to-ten age range to determine their readiness for school. If there is any doubt, it is usually better to wait. . . .
>
> There is no systematic body of research that indicates that young children who can be provided a good home will do as well or better if they go to preschool! The child who goes to school later, entering with his age-mates, nearly always comes out better academically, behaviorally, and socially.[37]

Other leading psychologists freely underscore the teaching quality of the home. David Elkind of the University of Rochester, Meredith Robinson of the Stanford Research Institute and William Rohwer of California-Berkeley join in suggesting that the home, provided it is good, is the best learning nest until near adolescence.[38]

6) *Home educators can monitor closely the pulse of their child's development and can with great effectiveness concentrate on the*

building of their child's vital self-respect. No one can be as concerned and as observant of a child's self-image development as a loving mother or father. No one can be as sensitive to a child's emotional hurts and needs as a concerned parent. Some parents apathetically relegate this task to influences outside the family. Others are not so much apathetic as they are naive and unaware. Either way, they often find there is a big price to pay down the road. Every child has his own individual needs and special concerns. Parents have the unique ability to become "specialists" on their child's overall growth and development like virtually no one else on the face of the earth.

7) *Home schoolers are not exposed to the "spillover" that can permeate private schools due to societal contamination.* Many children are placed in private schools for improper reasons: they need discipline, they need a change of friends, to counteract bad home life, etc. But the net effect is that many private schools are getting some malcontents of public education, along with their values, language, and lack of discipline. While moral instruction admittedly receives higher priority in private schools, they have not been left untainted with confused societal mores. Young children, in particular, are susceptible to moral confusion.

In addition, many private school teachers hold the same views as their public counterparts. I have talked with Christian teachers who ardently hold to the teaching of evolution. Tainted by secular humanism and liberal continuing education courses, some teachers have slowly dismissed doctrines, values, and beliefs they at one time cherished so highly. Others have begun using faulty and ineffective methodologies used in the public school system.

Curriculum is also a concern. Some parochial schools use the same textbooks the school district uses. I have witnessed private schools using the same humanistic texts you would find in the state-funded elementary school down the road.

8) *Home schoolers enjoy a unique educational freedom because they are not confined by time and space barriers.* Conventional schools follow a rigid time structure that does not allow for a wide variety of family learning experiences in the daytime. Only by pulling them out of classes can this be accomplished. For home educators, however, every hour of every day is a learning opportunity. Home educators do have to maintain a carefully defined structure in the home, but they can also allow for more flexibility than a conventional classroom setting. That is why "no school room can match the simplicity and power of the

home in providing three-dimensional, first-hand education. The school, not the home, is the substitute. . . ."[39]

It is conceded that not every home can provide an atmosphere conducive to quality home schooling. A good home combined with the parental ingredients of love, concern, and responsibility are essential. However, I can say that more homes could provide these advantages if they but give themselves half a chance. Are home educators qualified? The general impression most parents are left with today is that the best teaching is done in the classroom. This is a myth, primarily manufactured by those who are protecting their own jobs, by parents who are rationalizing because they want to get their children out from underneath their feet, and by people who simply do not know better. But in fact, any normal parent with a little curricular help can start his child on paths of competence which few classroom teachers can match.[40] It will require the realignment of priorities, but the benefits in the long run are tremendous.

FIVE

The "How" Of Home Schooling

T hough home schooling requires no special education or expertise, there are some practical considerations that make it easier to carry out. In this chapter we want to take a look at the "how" of home schooling. Parents who follow the few simple guidelines outlined here will find that home schooling is not only within their ability to carry out, but immensely rewarding as well.

Goals and Objectives

The first area to look at is that of setting your goals and objectives. Having no goals and objectives is like trying to sail a ship without a rudder or like taking a trip without a destination. God's Word says, "We should make plans counting on God to direct us" (Proverbs 16:9, TLB). The simple fact is, your child can only go where you take him. If you do not know where you are taking your child educationally, how will you know when or even if you have arrived? A goal is an end toward which your effort is directed, while an objective is a short-range step you take to ensure the meeting of your longer-range goal.

Setting goals and objectives should include three things. First, your goals should be *clearly defined*. Foggy or unclear goals only lead to frustration and confusion. In fact, they are really not goals at all—they are only ideas or wishes. Be specific with your educational goals. For example, what basic knowledge, skills, attitudes, and godly character traits would you like your children to develop? What Biblical doctrines and concepts would you like them to learn? What are your academic goals for each subject? I'm not talking about daily/weekly lesson plans or objectives here, but the identifying of knowledge, concepts, abilities, and character traits you would like for your child to grasp by year's end. You may want to start with only one-year goals at first, and later add five, ten, and beyond.

Academic goals can be easily assessed through the use of annual standardized testing. Other goals like the development of character traits and the child's love for God cannot be tested and hence must be appraised in the parent's heart. Do not let goal-setting frighten you. It is not as hard as it sounds, and with time you will grow to be a master of goal-setting. Many publishers of structured curriculums will provide academic goals for you. This is of tremendous help to the new home educator. Further, every state educational agency publishes the essential elements for each subject for grades K-12. These can often be obtained discreetly through a public or private school. Such a guidebook may help you in your academic planning. Do not let planning and goal-setting overwhelm you. It should be a tool, not an albatross around your neck.

Very important! List your goals in order of importance. Spend most of your teaching time on the subjects or attitudes of highest priority. When all is said and done, what is it exactly that you want your child to learn? What knowledge and attitudes do you want your child to carry with him throughout life? Your priorities should be determined by God's Word, and God's Word places its greatest emphasis on the development of love towards God and man. There are some goals that will require an indefinite time limit to fulfill. For example, certain character traits or attitudes may take several years to sprout and a lifetime to properly develop. Though they are crucial in the goal-planning process, they must remain flexible and in accordance with the child's age and spiritual maturity. Remember that teaching should not be confined to the classroom, but is also a life experience.

Secondly, goals and objectives are best when they are *put into writing*. A fact of human nature is this: unless you write your goals out, your chances of achieving them are very slim. Putting them in writing will do five things: 1) it solidifies them in your own mind and makes them more real; 2) it shows your seriousness; 3) it helps you to get organized; 4) it makes you feel better about yourself; and 5) it makes your teaching much easier. You only need to write your goals out once a year, making occasional minor revisions if they are needed. Your goals need not become so detailed that they become a drudgery, but they should road-map your desired educational destination for your child. Most teacher's guides will supply daily/weekly academic objectives to help you meet your goals, saving you from detailed scope and sequence work and complex lesson planning. Some publishers will even provide a coordinated master plan which integrates all of your subjects for you. Get all the help and advice you can from publishers and friends, but ultimately let your goals be in manuscript from your own pen. The reason is simple: personally written goals help you sort out your priorities and make adaptations to fit your child's individual need. This is one of the unique advantages of home schooling. Below is a sample of some written annual goals for a typical first-grader. Notice how they give direction and steer a course for the year.

Goals

Character
- Learn the names of the different types of godly character.
- Concentrate on the character development of love, attentiveness, and patience.
- Learn how the different character traits were demonstrated in the life of Jesus.
- Encourage the importance of character-building over all other types of knowledge and skills.

Bible
- Learn the key characters of both Old and New Testament.
- Learn the books of the Bible.
- Learn to differentiate between key Old and New Testament stories.
- Start on a basic Scripture memory plan.

Reading
- Learn the letters of the alphabet in their proper order.
- Learn consonant sounds in initial, medial, and final positions.
- Learn long and short vowel sounds.
- Learn "r" controlled vowel sounds.
- Learn vowel digraphs.
- Learn initial and final consonantal blends.
- Learn basic sight words.
- Learn elemental reading practices.
- Learn to answer basic questions about stories they have read.

Math
- Learn to count to 100 (also by multiples of 2, 5, and 20).
- Gain sight recognition of numerals 0-100.
- Learn to distinguish numerical order.
- Know how to distinguish numerals being greater than, less than, or equal to.
- Learn basic addition and subtraction facts of numerals 1-100.
- Learn place value in a three-digit number.
- Learn to tell time by the hour and half hour.
- Be able to solve simple story problems of addition and subtraction.
- Learn the value of a penny, nickel, dime, quarter, and half-dollar.
- Learn numerical word symbols (1-100).

Writing
- Learn how to write manuscript in both upper and lower case.
- Learn how to hold pencil/pen in the proper way.
- Learn to judge size and form of letters.
- Learn to write simple sentences neat and legibly.

Science
- Learn what science is: finding things out.
- Learn that God's Word is the ultimate source of all truth.
- Learn what the five senses are and how we use them.
- Learn about weather and seasons.
- Learn about basic scientific classification.
- Learn good health habits.

History
- Learn what history is and what it teaches us.
- Learn that God's Word is the source of historical fact on the original creation of the world and the condition of man.
- Learn basic facts about home, church, community, and country.
- Learn the importance of Thanksgiving, Christmas, and Easter.
- Learn about patriotism.
- Learn the importance of the flag and the Pledge of Allegiance.
- Learn that individuals and families are the building-blocks of society.

Objectives

Short-range objectives should work towards the achievement of your long-range goals. Below are sample objectives you might have during the course of a one-week period for the subject of Bible.

This week we will:
* Memorize John 3:16.
* Read/tell the story of Saul's conversion.
* Have them explain what salvation is.
* Complete Bible worksheets on pages 23-29.
* Complete Bible craft on Paul.

Or these weekly objectives for the subject of Math:
* Count out loud by 10's to 100.
* Go through sample addition problem on board.
* Complete workbook exercises on pages 8-15.
* Work on hour identification on clock face.

Goal- and objective-setting will bring overall organization to the teaching process and direction to your school year. Without this essential phase of planning, home education will be very difficult to carry out.

Thirdly, goals and objectives should *be achievable*. If you set goals for yourself or your child that are unrealistic or unachievable, both of you will become frustrated with home schooling. If you sense one of your goals is too broad or too difficult, don't be afraid to change or amend it. Goals are not meant to bind you—they are meant to free you—by giving you purpose, direction, and guidance.

Organization

Tied to and connected with setting goals and objectives is that of organizing yourself for effective home schooling. Every task is easier when you are organized. Home schooling is no exception. Good organization will make teaching easier for you and help your child maintain a strong learning interest. Further, it will eliminate many unnecessary behavioral problems. There are six logical areas home educators need organization in.

First, you need to organize your *time*. Decide on how much time you plan to devote to sit-down, academic learning and how much time for nonacademic or life-experience learning. Both kinds are educationally important since learning occurs through both mediums. Though the time period for academic learning will vary with grade level and individual child ability, a good suggestion would be to allow for approximately two to three hours a day. Life learning should take place continually, with every remark, activity, and duty becoming a form of learning. Adjust sit-down academic time requirements according to your child's needs and age.

Never compromise regular teaching time on important subjects. Some subjects allow for more flexibility than others (i.e., science). Other subjects do not (i.e., character development, learning to read and write, Scripture memory). On crucial subjects never allow yourself to get in the habit of saying, "I'll teach it if I have time left over." You will discover that left-over time will never come.

It is critical to avoid or minimize "time leaches." That is, those activities which quickly consume precious minutes and hours. Here are a few time leaches: unnecessary phone conversations, television viewing, overcommitments outside the home (recreational, civic, church, etc.), and excessive extracurricular activities. There are many other time wasters that disguise themselves in a multitude of ways. Beware of them or frustration will soon be knocking on your back door. Let me also be straightforward on a related point; except in extreme emergencies or justifiable financial necessity, mothers who home school should not work outside the home. It is unfair to the children who depend on your daily attention and guidance.

Not only should you decide on how much time, but also when this will occur in your daily schedule. Early morning right after breakfast is preferable. If your schedule makes this impossible, set a time of day that will work best for you and your child. The key here is to be consistent. Routines have both pros and cons, but my home schooling experience has taught me the value of routine maintenance. Routines help both you and your child to know what is expected and when. However, caution should be exercised not to be so rigid that the value of home school flexibility is totally destroyed.

The second area of organization is the *determination of a place*. Anything that helps your child's learning environment is an educational asset. Getting a specific place will help your child make the learning identification he needs in a home environment. Some home educators establish a certain room for instruction, purchasing school desks, a chalk or marker board, and a flag. All these are helpful, but none are absolutely necessary. Many with great success use nothing more than their kitchen table. Whatever place you choose, make sure that it has good lighting and is relatively free from bothersome and unnecessary distractions.

A third area you should organize yourself in is in *curriculum and supplies*. Choosing a curriculum is one of the more crucial decisions you will make in the area of home schooling. Look carefully at the curriculum of veteran home schoolers before you buy your own. Talk with them and ask about its strengths and weaknesses. Learn all you can before ordering. Many larger communities will sponsor home school book fairs which will expose you to a multitude of publishers and their educational wares. Here are some of the things you should consider in choosing a curriculum.

1) Is it Christocentric?
2) Is it well-organized for both the teacher and the child?
3) Was it designed for individual or group instruction?
4) Are daily/weekly lesson plans available?
5) If all your subjects are chosen from the same publishing house, does the publisher offer a master plan which coordinates the teaching of all subjects?
6) In reading curriculum, does it teach true phonics or "phony" phonics?
7) Does it undergird solid morality and godly character?
8) Does it have a proven track record among other home educators?

Below are some things to be on guard against when selecting curriculum. Watch for material which:

1) has either overt or covert infiltration of humanism.
2) is lean or skimpy on student/teacher interaction.
3) is morally or spiritually offensive.
4) overly emphasizes worksheets/busywork.
5) uses look-say reading methodology.
6) offers little or no teaching assistance.
7) is poor on subject coordination (applies only to those who go with one publisher for all subjects).
8) is hard to cost-justify (inexpensive material which teach the same information is often available).

It is also important to organize your supplies. Have a specific place for commonly used items like textbooks, scissors, glue, pencils, paper, crayolas, water paints, etc. Your child will enjoy knowing where to find these items and helping you keep them neat and orderly. Many parents have plastic trays to hold supplies for the younger students of the family.

A fourth area home educators should organize in is *teamwork*. By teamwork I mean the maximum use of available resources in the home. Any project can become burdensome if it is left in the hands of only one person. Mom only has twenty-four hours in a day, and that never seems to be enough. Housework, meal preparation, and general child care make many time demands on her. However, the home can be a rich place to draw resources from. It is these resources we want to consider here. The available resources are Dad, Mom, and children. Sounds simple, doesn't it? Dad, as head of the household, carries the ultimate responsibility for the proper training of his children. Since most Dads must work full-time to supply the family's needs, he usually delegates the primary day-to-day teaching responsibilities to Mom. She brings the consistency that is needed in order to maintain a place of learning. But Mom can't do it all alone. So she calls on the assistance of Professor Dad.

It is very important for Dad to choose a subject or subjects he can be involved in, especially but not exclusively those which are spiritual in nature. Dad should teach or at least participate in the teaching of either a Bible or a character development course. These courses can easily fit around Dad's work schedule and can be taught in the evenings or on weekends. As the family priest, spiritual responsibility should never be relinquished. Dads are specifically instructed, "Fathers . . . bring them (your children) up in the training and instruction of the Lord" (Ephesians 6:4). Other subjects which he could become involved with are those which require teaching only two or three times a week, like science, history, or physical education. His participation in the teaching process will not only ease the burden of Mom "doing it all," but it will show his support of and authority over the home schooling process.

Moms are an essential part of the team. In most homes she is usually responsible for the bulk of day-to-day teaching responsibilities. In addition to Dad's, she often finds help and encouragement at local support groups and from other home schooling moms. Without a doubt, home schooling does take time and a deep commitment, but the fruits are worth the effort. Energy limitations mandate that priorities be set as you will not have time for everything. This is especially true for moms with younger children. Often it means the temporary acceptance of less-than-perfect housekeeping conditions. Dads need to give special empathy in this area and help out as much as possible. It is all part of teamwork.

Children also serve as a member of the team. Since younger children naturally imitate the behavior and attitudes of their older siblings, the latter become very valuable as teaching assistants. Hence, home educators will want to utilize them as much as possible. Older brothers and sisters convey surprising amounts of basic knowledge and skills. They can help answer questions, explain directions or teaching concepts, and model independent study habits, attitudes, and character traits they themselves have mastered. But older children should never become an educational substitute for the parents, as that would cheat the younger ones out of essential time they need with Mom and Dad and hinder their learning. In addition, every child should be expected to learn and assume domestic responsibilities like washing dishes, sorting clothes, meal preparation, sewing, etc. Sometimes we feel that it's easier and faster to carry out home tasks ourself. But in the long run, the time investment you make to spread out these responsibilities will make your home more domestically efficient, while serving to instruct in important practical skills as well.

The whole family gains by utilizing the team teaching concept. Both Mom and Dad's work is made much easier, younger children are given extra guidance and attention, and the older children have their own learning and awareness of others reinforced. Teamwork builds mutual cooperation and respect in the educational process as well as family camaraderie, unity, and love.

Related to team teaching and yet different is the fifth area of organization. Home educators with two or more children must organize for *multilevel teaching*. Teaching children of various ages or grade levels requires a little extra planning, but it is by no means an impossible task. Since all children need time and attention, you may at times wish you had six arms and could be three places at once. However, organized management will allow you to make educational progress while keeping everyone happy most of the time. Though challenges will still arise, you can make multilevel teaching much easier by following two basic rules.

Rule number one is to teach jointly as many subjects as possible. Science, physical education, history, and character development are all examples of subjects which will frequently allow this. Science projects and experiments can easily become a family endeavor with great enjoyment and satisfaction. Think how much fun the family could have on the subject of weather.

For example, while younger children are learning to distinguish between the basic weather conditions of hot and cold, dry and wet, windy and still, the older children can be making instruments that scientifically measure wind speed and direction (i.e., wind sock, weather vane). Physical education classes can be a joint venture that builds both a spirit of competition and co-operation. Exercise and learning good health practices are more enjoyable in a warm family environment and can be easily taught on a multi-age basis. There are subjects where a younger child cannot really understand what is going on but still enjoys working side by side with big brother or sister. For example, a kinder-gartener may not understand second-grade math, but may still enjoy writing random numbers on a sheet of paper while the older student works. The key to combined grade teaching is cognizance of the different attention spans and levels of comprehension in your children, while adjusting your expectations accordingly.

Rule number two is simply this: at times where joint teaching is not an option, learn to productively divide your time and attention. For example, an older child should be assigned lessons conducive to independent work, while a younger child needs one-on-one tutoring. You can expect a first- or second-grader to occupy more time and attention since you are laying for them the groundwork for all future educational advancement. By occasionally checking in on the more mature scholars, time will be kept available to those minds which presently demand more personal attention. By emulating your example, older children will learn how to manage and efficiently occupy their own time when you are temporarily inaccessible. This in itself will greatly help them towards autonomous evaluation of the varying circumstances of life and give them a healthy dose of personal discipline to boot. Naturally, you will want to be continually sensitive to the older child's feelings and needs.

The sixth area home educators want to be organized in is *evaluation*. Parents should set intervals of evaluation in order to appraise their own effectiveness and their child's academic progress. For the parents, testing manifests the extent to which their goals are being reached. Testing for the child reveals his academic strengths and weaknesses.

Evaluation procedures can be both formal and informal. Formal testing involves the use of commonly accepted standardized testing instruments like the Iowa, California, and Stanford Achievement Tests. Informal testing is that which is either supplied by curriculum publishers (examination booklets with keys) or that which is personally written or designed. Home educators are strongly encouraged to *formally test their children once a year, maintaining a file of the test results*. Parents do not need to submit the results to anyone, except where required for legal or academic purposes (i.e., answering truancy allegations in a court of law, or entering a school or university). Such testing will demonstrate your child's academic progress and be available if ever needed.

Formal testing can be carried out three ways. First, several home schooling parents can band together, hiring a certified proctor to administer it. Second, a certified teacher can administer it privately. Third, home educators can have their child tested at a local Christian school. Not only do tests promote learning by stimulating study, but they also help students with "recall," which enhances the memory process. Testing, therefore, is just another tool in the educational process.

There are two cautions regarding testing however. First, testing should not be used primarily for peer comparison. A hidden danger lurks therein which can cause parents to unfairly judge their success and effectiveness solely on test results. A child's self-worth can also be negatively affected by an overemphasis on test results. That is why wise parents judge their success in light of their educational goals. They realize that test results do not always give the whole picture. Some very bright children test poorly. In addition, formal testing only measures the area of academics. It cannot measure the heart or the soul. It is better to view test results as just one piece in the whole evaluative pie. Parental standards of success should be based on many factors, including comparison with your own educational goals, general observations of a child's daily/weekly academic performance, growth of his overall self-esteem, and development of godly character. All these factors, along with test results, give a more accurate picture of what is going on in your child.

A second caution regarding testing is this: remember that the most important kind of evaluation comes from within the child himself. A child should learn to look within his own mind, heart, and soul and make an evaluation of his progress. He should also learn to assess his priorities. Show your child the importance of making evaluative determinations based on God's Word. Guide him to ask questions like these: "Who am I in God's eyes? What is my purpose and role in the world? Am I moving steadily towards that purpose? Am I making spiritual progress, growing in my love for God? Am I giving my best in everything I do, including my schoolwork?" When a child is able to answer these kinds of questions, then he is able to more readily evaluate his pursuit of academic objectives and take the appropriate action.

We should watch for two extremes in the area of testing: avoiding it altogether and overemphasizing it. Evaluation is a necessary part of the education process. So learn to make testing an enjoyable and pleasant experience for both you and your child. You will find it carries its own reward.

In sum, planning and coordination is the home educator's best friend. Parents who organize their time, place, curriculum, teamwork, multilevel teaching, and evaluative procedures will find that home schooling is not a difficult endeavor. It may be challenging at times, but it is always worthy of your best effort. Sure, you will make mistakes, but you will learn by them as well. Part of home schooling, like parenting, involves some trial and error. When you make an error in judgment, you will find your child is quite understanding and accommodating. Perfection is not required of home educators, but a measure of organization is. And with it you will find remarkable success.

The Importance of Character Education

The most important area of education is not the three R's, science, government, or even Bible history. No, the most important area of instruction is the development of godly character. It is the precious foundation-stone on which all other learning is built. If a person has great intellectual knowledge but little godly character, his life will not have much positive impact upon the world in which he lives. His life will become nothing more than a sandcastle, here today and gone tomorrow. It is true that a child must grow physically, mentally, emotionally, and socially, but the most important growth of all is spiritual.

By *character* I mean those qualities and virtues that emanate from the heart of Almighty God and make this world a better place to live in. They comprise but are not limited to: love, joy, peace, patience, kindness, goodness, gentleness, faithfulness, self-control, honesty, industry, initiative, obedience, attentiveness, thankfulness, meekness, diligence, friendliness, perseverance, a forgiving nature, etc. These are the traits that make a person complete and ready for life.

Character building requires a fear (godly respect) and love

for God. Wise Solomon said, "The fear of the Lord is the beginning of knowledge, but fools despise wisdom and discipline" (Proverbs 1:7). It must be sought diligently as for a treasure. Again Solomon says, "If you look for it as for silver, and search for it as for hidden treasure, then you will understand the fear of the Lord and find the knowledge of God" (Proverbs 2:4, 5). When a child receives Jesus as his personal Savior, he is born again spiritually into the kingdom of God. At this point, he starts on a lifelong spiritual growth process. Hence, development of godly character is the most important fruit to nurture in your child's life. It also happens to be the most difficult and demanding to instill. Why? Because the world, the flesh, and the Devil all fight and rebel ferociously against the inculcation of godly character. Paul said, "For our struggle is not against flesh and blood, but against the rulers, against the authorities, against the powers of this dark world and against the spiritual forces of evil in the heavenly realms" (Ephesians 6:12). These demonic forces are continually vying for the control seat of your child's heart and soul. They want nothing more than to rob him of his love for God and the character that His Spirit gives.

Since godly character springs from a deep relationship with Jesus Christ, you must teach your child to pray, and to read and commit to memory the Scriptures, and model for him as a Christian witness, teach him the importance of obedience to God's Word, and seek out fellowship with like-minded Christians. Your child must be taught to love God and to daily seek after Him with all his heart. As your child develops a deep and abiding relationship with Jesus Christ, he will be enabled to grow in divine character.

The important thing for parents to know is that true education should begin with, be centered around, and end with their child's love for God and the development of Christian character. This is both the origin and apex of all knowledge. Home educators have the rewarding advantage of giving it the priority it is due.

Teaching by Example

There is an old saying that goes like this: "What you do speaks so loudly that I can't hear what you say." There is truth evident herein. Children learn more by what they see than by what they hear. Well-intentioned parents often talk about the importance of solid values and Christian character but have a lifestyle that is inconsistent with what they teach. Parents must learn that how they live is far more important than what they say. For example, if a father tells his son that personal devotions are important, and yet he himself is never seen praying or reading his Bible, which carries the greater weight? If a mother tells her daughter that internal beauty is more important than external, yet spends excessive time and money on cosmetic enhancements, what has she really "taught"? If parents tell their children that TV viewing is a waste of time, and yet themselves spend hours in front of it, what do the children really learn? "Monkey see, monkey do," so to speak. Guard yourself against empty words by practicing what you teach. The best and most lasting form of childhood education comes by the observation of parental example.

Children can grow cognitively or intellectually without growing spiritually. That is why children can easily parrot beliefs and values their parents want to hear without believing it in their own heart. For example, a child can recite John 3:16 and yet not know personally the God of love described therein. He can recite Ephesians 4:32 and still be mean and unforgiving to his brothers, sisters, and playmates. Satan's work is very subtle here. Like adults, children can mimic Christian behavior but still be spiritually lukewarm. Do not look merely for intellectual recitation of values and beliefs. Rather, look for complete transformation of character and lifestyle which conforms to the will of God.

It all comes down to what your educational goals and priorities are. Do you want a child who is very intelligent but who lacks beauty of character? Or do you want a child who not only knows the three R's but loves and honors God with his life? Both lifestyles are learned. One reason we have many problems with public schoolchildren these days is because of the so called "wall of separation between church and state," a phrase found nowhere in the U.S. Constitution. It was never the intention of the Founding Fathers to expel Christianity from the schoolhouse. However, many parents have been propagandized into thinking their children should get head-knowledge in school and heart-knowledge in church. But in reality the two go hand in hand. If they are separated, peer pressure and influence throughout the week will teach significantly more values than parents can deprogram on evenings and weekends or that the pastor can unteach on Sunday mornings. This creates unreconcilable value contamination. The big advantage of home education is the ability to teach Christian values by example and through interdisciplinary coordination with the Word of God. This is how godly education takes place.

There is one thing that is essential to effectively educate your child unto godliness. You must live what you teach. You must be what you ask your child to become. David said, "I will walk in my house with blameless heart" (Ps. 101:2). You must set the godly example yourself while orally teaching him to do it. In addition to your own example, you must also pray for him. Every Christian parent should spend time on their knees seeking divine guidance and protection for their child. How else can they fulfill the command of Ephesians 6:4, where parents are commanded to bring up their children in the nurture and admonition of the Lord? Many hours of behind-the-scenes prayer is a crucial part of the educational process. Diligently ask God to give you the wisdom to present knowledge in an effective way.

Learning is a continual process where a child absorbs information from many sources. All five senses are employed in the process. But there are many things Christian parents do not want their child to emulate. Because of this, a child's environment should be well-regulated. Here are some key areas where children can be negatively affected by their environment:

1) television viewing.
2) the friends they keep.
3) the music they listen to.
4) the books they read.
5) the forms of entertainment they engage in.
6) the places they are allowed to go.
7) church (those which are cold, unexciting, and dull).
8) the toys and possessions they are allowed to collect.

An element of control and/or restraint must be placed in each of these eight areas. Where the home is school, the T.V. is of special concern. Generally speaking, television viewing is a poor use of time. Unfortunately it comprises a very large chunk of time in American households. Most homes would be far better off without a T.V. set. Without television, more time would be available for family communication and interaction, crucial time that is all but lost in modern American society. At the very least, TV viewing should be limited to a fixed number of hours with programming strictly censored. This would teach your children both discipline and restraint. But remember, children learn by example.

Discipline and Manners

Two of the attributes that are regrettably absent among so many children today are discipline and manners. Home educators have the opportunity to reinstate these qualities that are personally and culturally valuable. Like every other form of knowledge, discipline and manners are a learned behavior and must be taught.

When children are small, their world must be structured and ordered for them. But as they grow they should be taught the importance of self-discipline. Discipline is required in the following areas: spiritual, physical, mental, and social. A child needs to learn the spiritual value of daily personal devotions and the danger of its neglect. Physically, he should be taught the right kinds of foods to eat, how to exercise properly, and good hygienic procedures. He should learn the consequences of eating junk food and physical inactivity. Mentally, he must be taught that knowledge requires a price. He must take time to read, learn, and ask questions beyond what is absolutely necessary. Socially, he must learn to discern those places and friends that are good and those which are not. He needs to learn when he has socialized enough.

There is a thread, however, which ties all four of these areas together. A child needs to become master of his time. Time is a very precious commodity, and we have all been dealt the same daily amount. Yet it is so fleeting, so easy to waste. Scripture says we should be "making the most of every opportunity, because the days are evil" (Eph. 5:16). Some will accomplish great things in their life with the amount they are allotted. Others will achieve little or nothing. Learning to be the master of time requires learning how to set priorities. To gain discipline in this area will place a child in the top 1 percent of Americans. But here again, he learns by example.

Manners are another forgotten courtesy in modern life. How refreshing it is to be around children who have been taught graceful table manners, politeness, respect for elders, and proper social etiquette. Jesus always exhibited the best of manners regardless of where He went or what He did. Teach your child to emulate His example. No one likes to be around a rude, spoiled, insensitive brat. Children will become like this if parents allow it and do not instruct otherwise. The Bible says, "A child left to itself disgraces his mother" (Prov. 29:15b). Bad manners is not something a child grows out of, but something he grows up with. Do your child a great service by teaching him thoughtfulness, graciousness, amiability, and excellence of behavior. It will help him go a long way in life. Remember, your children and their manners are a reflection of you.

Scheduling

We have already talked about the importance of goals and objectives. Now we want to talk about structuring your days and weeks to accommodate them. It takes a while to set up a schedule that works for your family school, but once done it will only require infrequent and minor alterations. At first it may seem a bit rigid, but with time you will learn where your flexibility lies. You can pattern your own schedule following the sample below or even design your own. The main thing is that it works for you and helps you accomplish your goals and objectives.

Suggested Weekly Schedule for a First Grader

TIME	MON. TUES. WED. THURS. FRI.
7:00- 8:00	Rise, morning prayers, breakfast, make bed, get dressed, brush teeth (and any other morning routines)
8:00- 8:15	*Opening*: Prayers, Pledge of Allegiance, songs of praise, discuss day's schedule ————
8:15- 8:45	Bible instruction————————————
8:45- 9:30	Math ———————————————
9:30- 9:45	Break——————————————
9:45-10:15	Reading ———————————————
10:15-10:45	Language Skills—————————
10:45-11:00	Handwriting —————————————
11:00-12:00	Arts and Crafts—————————
12:00- 1:00	Lunch/Recess————————————
1:00- 1:30	Quiet Time—————————————
1:30- 3:15	Living skills (domestic skills, manners, gardening, etc.), field trip
3:15- 4:00	Gymnastics
4:00	Piano

Evening Instruction by Dad

TIME	MON.	TUES.	WED.	THURS.	FRI.
7:00-7:45	Character Lesson	Science Lesson	Character Lesson	History Lesson	
7:45-8:15	Storytime	Storytime	Storytime	Storytime	Storytime

Field Trips and Extracurricular Activities

Field trips are an important and exciting part of education. Whether it be the library, ballet, bakery, museum, historical site, or a manufacturing plant, children will always be elated with these memorable experiences. Make sure you count field trips as a part of your overall school program. Mom and Dad may be the tour guides or the children may travel with a group of area home schoolers. Either way, these educational excursions help make the learning process more meaningful. Plan on having at least one field trip a month. Also provide some way for the children to record these trips to help reinforce learning. Photographs, written reports, and picture booklets are several ways this can be accomplished.

Extracurricular activities are also important but should not be overemphasized. You may want your child to take voice or instrument lessons through a local music instructor. Or you may take advantage of gymnastics, swimming, ballet, art, or ceramics offered at a nearby YMCA or city recreation center. There are many other extracurricular possibilities. Like field trips, remember to count extracurricular activities as a part of your overall school program. Not only will your child learn through these activities, but they will provide a good opportunity for outside social stimulation. City recreation centers and YMCAs provide these services at a very reasonable cost.

Grading

Letter grading is optional in a home school setting. The best advice here is simply this: use letter grading if it helps stimulate educational growth, and dispense with it if it causes anxiety or a negative learning environment. Grades, like testing procedures, are to be used as an educational tool. It is suggested that you make comments on the top of their school papers that give praise or positive reinforcement for work well done. Children respond favorably to this.

Length of School Year

Since the emphasis on home schooling should be on "full-life" education, do not allow yourself to be hemmed in by the nine-month public school cycle. One of the unique strengths of educating at home is being able to maximize on year-round learning. Summer is a good time to do outdoor experiments or to learn the principles of gardening. Vacations are also a terrific opportunity to learn. We should not think of education as a nine-month-a-year activity. Instead, plan for it to be a continual learning experience on the child's road to maturity and preparation for life.

Some parents choose to parallel their academic and holiday scheduling to that of the local school system, believing this helps the child to avoid feelings of oddity while giving his mind a rest. This is O.K. as long as you encourage the educational process to continue. Other parents feel that teaching year-round takes a great deal of pressure off them since they have a longer time to complete course requirements. Whichever way you choose, remember that children are learning even in the summer months. In addition, certain areas like character education and Scripture memory should never cease.

Making the Transition to a Traditional School

Should the time ever come when you feel it necessary to place your child in a traditional school, try at all costs to make it a Christian one. A Christian school will best complement the time and effort you have invested in your child over the years. Most parents find that their children are academically ahead of their peer counterparts. Formal testing will help you to make the proper ascertainment here. Unless the results show significantly otherwise, start your child in the grade where you left off. For example, if your child just finished fifth grade at home, plan to start him in the sixth grade come the new school year. Work with the school admissions counselor to do what is best for your child and to make the adjustment as easy as possible. If you have been his teacher for the past five years, who will know better than you? Take along the records you have kept over the years, but do not show them unless absolutely necessary. Remember, they are your property. Again, most transitions go quite smoothly. When all is said and done, I think you will find you did a far better job of teaching than you gave yourself credit for. Further, your child will have priceless memories to carry with him for a lifetime.

Independent vs. Satellite Schooling

Every home educator has two choices: teaching independently or going through a satellite or umbrella school. There are some practical advantages for home educators, especially new ones, who go through a satellite school. They guide you in selecting a curriculum, offer you teaching tips, and supervise formal testing instruments. Some will even grade homework lessons. All of them will maintain enrollment records which are available if transferring to another school. However, keep in mind that state education authorities may not accept the validity of such enrollment records or their compliance with compulsory attendance laws, especially if the school is located outside of your state. Don't expect a satellite school to be a fail-safe legal advocate. You may be sorely disappointed. Satellite schools which function by correspondence have a greater practical value than a legal one. However, many parents place high value on the accountability that a satellite school requires. If that and the other services described above would be helpful to you, and if it is worth the nominal fee they charge, by all means give them due consideration.

There may be a satellite school in your own state or even in your home town. Many are operated in connection with a local Christian school. If you elect the satellite method, it is advantageous to choose one nearby. All the services mentioned above are usually offered, except your child is not just a correspondence student. You can take your child in for certain classes, extracurricular activities, library usage, and other helpful benefits. Many will plan and coordinate local field trips for area home schoolers. Some states look more favorably at schools operating within their own boundaries, especially those having a physical campus with educational facilities.

Those who teach independently learn to depend on local support groups, newsletters, seminars, and other home schoolers for their guidance. Many independent educators received teaching experience under the auspices of a satellite school until they felt competent enough to go it alone. Others started independently from the word go. Independent teaching requires more organization but leaves the parents in complete control. Since parents are ultimately responsible for their children no matter which option they take, many want the freedom and flexibility that that control offers.

Conclusion

There is as much to say on the "how" of home schooling as there are parents who home school. Myriads of home-spun techniques, ideas, and practical applications are being created as you read. No book could include them all. Nor would it want to. What works well for one family might not work well for another. Much of the "how" of home schooling comes by: 1) praying for God's guidance and wisdom in all that you do; 2) modeling personally the behavior and lifestyle you want your child to learn; 3) employing a certain degree of trial and error while keeping your eyes fixed on predetermined goals; 4) designing a workable schedule which serves both your child's and family's needs; and 5) interacting with other home schooling parents on a regular basis. Remember that home schooling should be a continual learning process incorporating all of life's experiences. A great deal of learning takes place outside the classroom. Hence, supermarket shopping becomes a mathematical challenge for youngsters learning addition, subtraction, and percentages. The kitchen becomes a science lab. The workbench becomes a carpentry shop. A camping trip becomes a scientific encounter with nature. If you diligently apply the suggestions outlined in this chapter, and add creativity and love, you will be surprised at your abilities, talents, and educational effectiveness. But most important of all, teach your child to delight himself in the Lord and to acknowledge Him in all his ways. For that is a parent's highest achievement in life.

SIX

How
To Begin

W hat we do in life is determined by our priorities. The Bible makes crystal-clear that the godly upbringing of children should be the top priority of parents. Many parents, unfortunately, have higher priorities than their children: wealth accumulation, career development, material possessions, worldly friendships, etc. But the *top priority of parents should be their children*! According to Scripture, parents have four main duties in fulfilling this priority.

First, they are charged with surrounding their children with love and care. The core of all family life is composed of love, empathy, and self-giving. Jesus said that compassion towards children has its reward. *Secondly*, parents are required to provide for their children. This provision should incorporate the following: spiritual nurture, meeting of material necessities, and emotional understanding. By providing for your child in these areas, it will give him vitally-needed security, protection, companionship, and spiritual stamina. In order to accomplish this, parents obviously need to spend a great deal of time in the company of their children. *Thirdly*, parents are responsible for their overall instruction. This task is clearly and firmly placed upon the parents. It is implicit that even if others teach your child, you are still held accountable and must carry the prime responsibility for the results. Though this instruction should incorporate all critical subject matter, spiritual instruction should be the heart of all knowledge conveyed to the child. *Fourth*, parents are charged with the discipline of their children.

Biblical discipline calls for parents to give Scriptural guidance and correction, punishment for wrongdoing, praise for rightdoing, and to serve as an obedient model for the child. In essence, it means to raise a child in such a way that he displays loving obedience to God and parental authority, self-control, and responsibility. The results bring a blessing to the parents. The Bible says, "Discipline your son, and he will give you peace; he will bring delight to your soul" (Prov. 29:17).[1]

Some instruction finds its place and purpose in each one of these four parental duties, and explicitly in the third one. If you have decided to give home instruction serious consideration, rather than delegating that responsibility to others, then it is wise to heed four suggestions.

Four General Suggestions

Number One: Before you make any final decision *pray about it*. The Bible says, "They that seek the Lord understand all things" (Prov. 28:5, KJV). Seek out the wisdom of Almighty God to see if home schooling is for you. Home schooling is not for everyone. Many couples are concerned about their child's development and education. However, they may not be willing to give it the priority or make the sacrifice it often requires. In this case, home schooling would be an injustice to their children. Private Christian schooling then becomes your best alternative. (See Chapter 8.)

It must be said here that home schooling should be entered upon with the heartiest of Christian conviction. But what is Christian conviction? Unlike a preference, which is a religious belief subject to change, a conviction rests on an unshakable truth which one believes is ordained by God. For example, a conviction would be the belief that God ordained parents, not government, to be responsible for the education of their children. A conviction, therefore, is the very fabric of one's belief system. It is an unalterable Biblical truth you firmly believe is of divine origin.

Number Two: *Read, research, and familiarize yourself with the topic of home schooling*. The knowledge you gain will help confirm in your own mind that you have made a right decision. In addition, you will gain new insights and ideas about improving your home school. Books, magazines, and monthly newsletters will provide an almost unending source of current information. (A recommended reading list is provided at the end of this book.) These reading sources will give you detailed information about available curriculums, state laws, satellite schools, support groups, scheduling, spiritual training, plus many, many other topics.

Number Three: *Get in contact with a local home school support group or veteran home schooler*. These individuals can provide you with the emotional support necessary for getting started. In addition, they will be able to share valuable knowledge that only comes with experience. Talk with as many as possible. The Bible says, "Plans fail for lack of counsel, but with many advisors they succeed" (Prov. 15:22).

Number Four: *Your first year or two, go with a structured curriculum or satellite school*. Until you get the feel of home schooling, the whole experience can seem overwhelming. But this will pass. Soon you will grow to rely on divine guidance along with your own judgment and instincts. A satellite school can give you the organization and security that you at first may need.

Some Do's and Don'ts of Home Schooling

Some Don'ts!

1) *Don't* make any rash moves. Don't just yank your child out of school. Give yourself time to proceed in the most effective and productive manner. Try to keep a low profile so as not to draw attention to yourself or your child. This could cause embarrassment to both you and him.

2) *Don't* rush out and buy expensive curriculum. Before you invest in any curriculum, check out and familiarize yourself with the material other home schoolers in your area are using. Frequently you will find that you can obtain a very good curriculum without spending a great deal of money.

3) *Don't* be overly concerned about legal aspects. According to the United States Constitution, selecting your child's education alternatives is a fundamental parental right. Therefore, don't get exasperated about your state's interpretation of that right. Know what your state laws are, but don't let them cause you unnecessary worry.

4) *Don't* let your decision to home school be based on your child's acceptance of the idea. Many accept the idea immediately, but a few may require some time adjustment, especially those who are older when they start.

5) *Don't* get discouraged if others do not share your enthusiasm to home school. This is typical. Hence, the crucial reason to seek out and fellowship with other home schoolers.

Some Do's

1) *Do* explain to your child your reasons for home schooling. While it should not require his approval, he should have it explained to him in detail.

2) *Do* understand that home schooling requires a deep commitment. It is not something to be undertaken lightly or impulsively. The Bible says,

> "Suppose one of you, wants to build a tower. Will he not first sit down and estimate the cost to see if he has enough money to complete it? For if he lays the foundation and is not able to finish it, everyone who sees it will ridicule him, saying, 'This fellow began to build and was not able to finish'" (Luke 14:28, 29).

Count the costs and know what is involved. Understand that home schooling is a serious decision that requires a serious commitment. Your commitment will not only involve your time, but also your money, your emotions, your abilities, and your Biblical resolve.

Let's briefly consider just the monetary aspect. You will continue to pay local school taxes even though you choose an alternative education. Further, the current tax code is already biased against family life. This is a fact which results from cultural attitudes that are prevalent in contemporary American life. In the past twenty-five years we have witnessed the collapse of the cultural family wage, the emergence of a two-income family norm which structurally discourages marriage and children, a mounting antifertility incentive within Social Security, and the transference of the income tax burden onto families with children.[2] For example, Treasury analyst Eugene Steuerle has discovered a major shift between 1960 and 1984. During these years:

> . . . The average tax rate affecting single and married persons without children had not substantially changed. Yet the average tax rate of a couple with two children had climbed 43 percent; for a couple with four children, the increase was a staggering 223 percent. . . . The cause of this development was the steady erosion of the real value of the personal exemption combined with the rise in real income. If the exemption was to offset the same average percentage of income in 1984 as it did in 1948, it would have been worth $5,600 per person. Instead, it languished at $1,000 (indexed to inflation after 1984).[3]

The result is that traditional family life is monetarily discouraged by the Federal Government.

Home schoolers, as traditional families, will be challenged in this and in various other ways. To be sure, the metal of their commitment will be tested. That is why it must be solid. A few things home schoolers will face is: 1) a unique and demanding time commitment to their children's education; 2) inequitable tax laws that are biased against family life; 3) continued yet unfair tax support of public education; 4) friends and relatives who may criticize or ridicule what they don't understand; 5) and possibly confrontation with the interpretation of local and state compulsory attendance laws. Is it worth it? You bet it is! But a strong *commitment* must be there!

3) *Do* remember that there is a difference between religious conviction and religious preference. It is *conviction* that sets responsible home schoolers apart from the uncommitted. It is conviction that gives them their best legal prerogative.

4) *Do* expect to have both parents involved in home schooling. It must be a commitment to mutual involvement and support if you are to accomplish your best effectiveness.

5) *Do* expect to invest time. No matter what the product, quality craftmanship is best produced when it is afforded full attention. Similarly, parents must give home schooling the time it needs in order to produce quality results. Specifically, mothers who want to give home schooling their best and most serious effort should not work outside the home. Those couples who maintain that they need the extra money must reevaluate that decision in light of new priorities. Further, fathers must not expect the whole job to fall on Mom's shoulders. It is his responsibility to get involved and help in every way possible. This is part of "counting the cost."

6) *Do* get organized. Organization is crucial to successful home schooling. Good organization will permit you to do many of the other things that are also important to you.

7) *Do* have a good attitude. Your child will detect immediately any frustration or disinterest, which in turn will reflect in his desire to learn from you. Remember, your attitude is contagious.

8) *Do* be disciplined. Discipline is vital to your home schooling success. Set up a schedule for yourself and your child. Try to conform to certain times and places for study. Structure your day to give your child an hour or two of consistent tutoring daily.

9) *Do* be flexible. Though it sounds contradictory with the previous point, it is not. Remember, you are still a home school

and must make allowances for other children, phone calls, the doorbell, visitors, field trips, and other special events of educational interest, etc. None of these occurrences need to ruin your daily plans. Learn to have healthy flexibility.

10) *Do* have a family goal which continually keeps your priorities before your mind. How can one know if he has arrived at his destination if he does not know where he is going? A family purpose or goal is your road map to success. It not only helps you to know where you are going, but by revealing what is and is not important to you, your decision-making process becomes much easier.

The Goal of Education

In concluding this book it is important that we consider what the ultimate goal of all education is. The goal will determine the direction and presuppositions for the whole educational process. Historically, education has been provided with many purposes in mind. A summary of the educational goals of various individuals spanning the centuries follows:

1) Character, morality: Plutarch (Spartans), Herbart.
2) Perfect development: Plato, Rabelais, Montaigne, Comenius, Locke, Parker.
3) Happiness: Aristotle, James Mill.
4) Truth: Socrates.
5) Citizenship: Luther, Milton.
6) Mastery of nature: Bacon, Huxley.
7) Religion: Comenius.
8) Mental power, discipline: Locke, Van Dyke, Rendign.
9) Preparation for the future: Kant.
10) Habits: Rousseau, William James.
11) Unfolding: Froebel, Hegel.
12) Holy life: Froebel.
13) Interests: Herbart.
14) Knowledge: L. F. Ward.
15) Complete living: Spencer.
16) Culture, liberal education: Dewey.
17) Skill: Nathaniel Butler, E. C. Moore.
18) Inheritance of culture: N. M. Butler.
19) Socialization: W. T. Harris, Dewey.
20) Social efficiency: Dewey, Bagley.
21) Adjustment: Dewey, Rendign, Chapman, Counts.
22) Growth: Dewey.
23) Organization of experience: Dewey.

24) Self-realization: Dewey, Tufts.
25) Satisfying wants: Thorndike, Gates.
26) Insight: Gentile.[4]

As you can see, there are many different views on the goal of education. The question is, what is the Christian view? Let us first state what it should not be. The goal of education should not be the knowledge of facts in a particular subject matter, nor should it be mental discipline and the ability to think, nor the creative and/or spontaneous expression of problem solving, nor social adjustment and efficiency. Each of these things have their place, but for the Christian they should not be the ultimate goal of education. These are the goals of the secularist.

For the Christian, however, the goal of education is spiritual restoration. Dr. H. W. Byrne has stated it this way:

> The true aim of education for the Christian is redemptive. The purpose of education is to restore the image of God in man through Christ which leads to Christlike character and conduct. Integration can be attained only in this way. Such a person is one who finds all things centered in God, coming from God, existing for God, and evaluated by God. Subject matter is a means to this end. Such a person also will move out into society as a witness and work effectively to bring society to the ideal of the kingdom of God.[5]

Hence, the goal of education is to bring our children to God to be forgiven, renewed, and given purpose by Him. It is the transformation and growth of the child's body, mind, and spirit that they might serve God and live for Him. It is to so "excite and direct the self-activities of the pupil that he will volitionally strive for the best possible integration of personality on the human level," but directed toward the ultimate objective of the "perfect man in Christ."[6] This is the true goal of education!

SEVEN

Why Grandparents Should Support Home Schooling

I n talking with scores of home schoolers across America I have discovered that grandparents have a big impact on home schooling; some positive, some negative. Grandparents of home schoolers can do more to strengthen and encourage home educators than perhaps anyone else. Often they do not lend such support because they do not fully understand the reason and purpose of home schooling. In this chapter we want to look at ten reasons why grandparents should support those in their family who have decided to home school.

If your son or daughter has chosen to home school, it was a decision which demanded very careful consideration. More than likely, it was a decision that didn't come easy. Estimates indicate that about one in forty-four children are home schooled in this country. The very fact that they have decided to go against the educational numbers and the complacent tide of social acceptance shows their devout courage and boldness. Their desire to keep their child home shows their parental devotion and self-sacrifice. Grandparents should praise the priorities of offspring who show such concern and love for their children. Instead of pursuing a materialistic self-indulgence evident in much of modern society, your children have chosen to devote themselves to a very high calling. Many young people today are choosing not to have children because of the "bother and interference" they bring to their lifestyle. Others can't wait to shove them off to kindergarten, and even preschool to get them out from under their feet. The stalwart conviction of home educators shows their moral and spiritual backbone, which is a rare quality these days. In a hedonistic society whose hour of accountability is rapidly drawing nigh, home schoolers stand out as a value-centered elite.

How proud this should make the grandparents of home schoolers. Chances are, someone in your genealogical roots was home schooled with great success. You owe it to your son or daughter to consider the logic of the home schooling alternative. Below are ten reasons why grandparents should support their son or daughter's home schooling decision.

1) *You should support their decision because the education of American youth is still your responsibility.* No matter what your age or how long ago you graduated from school, the present generation is still your educational responsibility. Older Americans must help younger Americans experience quality learning. The future of this country rests in its young people. The strongest and most powerful army in the world is the army of youth, for there is not one position held in the world today that they will not hold tomorrow. Without your avid concern over our present educational crisis, the ideas our youth are embedded with today will one day surface in the form of unfair laws, burdensome taxation, and government interference. It has been said that "the hand that rocks the cradle rules the world." The question is, whose hand do you want it to be?

2) *You should support their decision if you believe in basic constitutional rights, which includes such freedoms as religious exercise, speech and belief, privacy, and parental liberty.* America was founded on a solid constitutional base which thus far has given its citizenry the greatest freedoms of any country in the world. However, if these precious freedoms are stepped on or choked out, America will lose its greatness. If the rights of someone else is violated, it won't be long before yours are too. Abraham Lincoln once said, "The philosophy of our educational system of today will be the philosophy of our government tomorrow." Home schoolers merely want to exercise their constitutional rights of religious exercise, speech and belief, privacy, and parental liberty. It is to your advantage to see that these rights are not denied them.

Should the unthinkable time ever arrive when the constitutional rights of home instructing parents is violated, what an exceedingly grim day it will be. Not only would it manifest the massive erosion of fundamental American rights, but also the regrettable extent of governmental control in family matters.

Should this ever occur, it is likely that persecution and/or stringent regulation of private Christian schools is not far behind.

3) *You should support their decision because you owe them an open-minded attitude towards educational alternatives.* The best American success stories have come from conscientious and innovative Americans who were given a fair chance. Did you ever embark on some new undertaking in life only to find yourself discouraged by closed-minded, negative-thinking people? Imagine how a home schooler must feel when he receives little or no encouragement from the ones he thought he could count on most, his family.

Do not take it as a personal insult if your son/daughter chooses to home school. They are not trying to depreciate the way you raised them, or reject the manner in which they were schooled. Times have changed, and in some areas not always for the better. What was once true about education is not necessarily true today. The point is, modern classroom education has not been achieving desirable results. Home schooling is one answer to the problem. Hence, do not take it as a personal affront to your own parentage.

4) *You should embrace their decision because your son/daughter needs your support.* No one can give your son/daughter emotional, spiritual, and psychological support quite like you. You have a unique opportunity to do what no one else can. The reverse is also true. No one can cause more emotional and psychological hurt. Home schooling is a challenging task that requires love and support. As their lifelong parents, it is your proper role to give it.

5) *You should embrace their decision because your grandson/granddaughter needs your support.* Grandchildren need support too. They are keenly aware of any criticism of their parents and their home schooling decision. Usually home schoolers abide by their decision to home educate even if their parents disapprove. This being the case, why not make your grandchild's home schooling experience as pleasant as possible. Get involved and be a part of something exciting.

6) *You should support their decision because home education has effectively proven itself.* The academic track record of home schoolers is spectacular. In fact, they average about 30 percentile points higher on standardized academic achievement tests than do classroom students. In addition to their superior academic performance, home schoolers evidence more creativity, enthusiasm, family-centeredness, submission to authority, and better manners and display higher moral values. Who would deny that these are admirable qualities? So why knock a good thing, particularly when it works so well given half a chance?

7) *You should support their decision because you value the building of character and godliness in children.* Home schooling builds character, the kind of character found in great leaders and inventors. People like George Washington, Benjamin Franklin, Alexander Graham Bell, Albert Einstein, and Sandra Day O'Connor are a few of the long list of home schoolers that we speak of. Character is what will set your grandchild apart from all the rest. Character is what will give him the ability to stand on his own two feet, to say no when he is asked to participate in something wrong. Character is that quality which gives him the ability to discern situations for himself and to make wise decisions.

Beyond that, home schooled children are taught godliness. How important is this to you? Do you want your grandchild brought up in the nurture and admonition of the Lord? If so, be cognizant of the fact that there is no better way to accomplish this than through home schooling.

8) *You should support their decision because it gives you a golden opportunity to participate in your grandchild's education.* Historically, grandparents have always been held in a place of high respect. They were looked up to and sought out for their sound wisdom, counsel, and advice. Much of this has been lost in our pleasure-seeking, me-first society. The elderly are shipped off to old folks' homes to be forgotten. Others have been persuaded by society that retirement is an end in itself. But home schooling attempts to bring back the wisdom and the teaching value of grandparents. The Bible says, "The glory of young men is their strength, gray hair the splendor of the old" (Prov. 20:29). Help your grandchild discover your honor and "splendor" by allowing him to learn from your valued experiences in life and to treasure them in his heart.

9) *You should support their decision because you don't want your grandchild to be another clone of educational failure.* The dismal track record of public schools is another reason you should support home education. When one third of our entire adult population (about sixty million) read very poorly or not at all, I think it's time we seriously examine our educational system. When science and math scores have shown a drastic drop over the past twenty years, it is time that we take notice. How big a sign do you need to see the failure of public education? More importantly, why encourage your grandchild's participation in a system that doesn't work?

10) *You should support their decision because you love your grandchild and want his highest good.* No one doubts your sincerity and love for your grandchildren. And here is the perfect opportunity to demonstrate it. Loving and responsible grandparents will support

and encourage any viable avenue of education which will promote their grandchild's highest good, no matter how different it may seem.

In conclusion, when we speak of supporting your son/daughter we do not mean passive acceptance and silent acknowledgment. The first way you can show support for home schooling is by reading up on the subject yourself. Find out everything you can about it. Secondly, avoid making comparisons with other granchildren, especially if they are negative in nature. Recognize that a home schooled child is not perfect; home schooling just allows their character and personality the opportunity to develop to its fullest potential. Be careful not to discriminate or judge them differently, unequally, or with greater scrutiny. Thirdly, support involves showing a genuine interest in home schooling by your attitudes, mannerisms, facial expressions, and words. A good way you can show genuine interest is to ask your son/daughter how you can become involved.

EIGHT

Choosing Other Private Education Alternatives

A s previously mentioned, home education may not be the best alternative for everyone. If after having read this book you feel that home schooling is not for you, conventional private schooling is still a strong choice. It is an extremely viable approach to learning which continues to keep education under the auspices of parental control. Parental involvement and control is, of course, the key. Most parents who consider the alternatives to public education are aware of the abuses being propagated in government-controlled schools. They want their child to be educated in an environment where he can maximize his learning potential and where their authority is not undermined. In these and other important areas, public schooling will never hold a candle to that which is available in the private sector. However, when private education is chosen, you still have some important choices to make. If you feel uncomfortable with the idea of home schooling, the following are your two best educational options.

Cottage Education

One option in the private school arena is cottage education. No book on this subject would be complete unless it gave due examination to the area where home schools dovetail with private schools. There are many creative options in childhood growth and learning. One of these options is *cottage education*. Cottage education is the cooperative teaching efforts among two or more families. It is the halfway point between conventional private schooling and home tutoring. For some who feel uneasy about single-family home schooling this may be an ideal solution.

Though the setting might be untypical of those found in conventional schools, cottage education essentially consists of several families banding together to form a private school. Properly initiated and convened, cottage schools can provide a warm and educationally stimulating environment. There are three main reasons why the cottage alternative is appealing. *First*, some parents feel more comfortable when they are not required to be the sole or primary teacher, even though they may agree with the enormous benefits available to those home tutored. Since teaching duties are shared or put up for hire, cottage education for the most part would alleviate this concern. *Secondly*, some parents desire to send their child to a conventional private or parochial school but are unable to afford the expensive tuition fees inherent therein. However, cottage schooling is able to accomplish much the same goals without the fiscal liability. Then *thirdly*, some parents prefer the student-teacher ratios available in home schools, but do not want the exclusive teaching duties that go with it. Here again, cottage schools may offer the perfect solution.

Cottage schools differ from traditional home schools in three main ways: number of pupils, location, and methodology. As for the *number of students*, cottage schools will usually have four to twelve students instead of the usual one to four found in the typical home schooling family. Though the number of pupils can exceed twelve, cottage education works best when it remains small.

Regarding *location*, cottage schools are often taught in a home environment. In such a setting, adequate space for each child must be given due consideration. Though several homes could be used for subject matter or age grouping, shifting locations should be kept to a minimum to avoid disruption and confusion. Or perhaps the student group could meet with regularity at the largest home, while changing only the parent teachers. If the instructional group is kept to a reasonable size, each student will benefit from the warm home environment and the opportunity to learn alongside other home schoolers.

A second locational possibility for cottage groups is to rent a room in a local church or private facility. Unless the premises are currently committed during the week, many churches will cooperate with cottage groups for a minimal amount of rent. Most Sunday school rooms are adequately supplied with chairs, proper lighting and ventilation, a chalk or marker board, and nearby restroom facilities. In addition, the neutral location will accommodate a more conducive learning environment when larger class numbers are involved. When parents work in unison, they can also afford to buy certain equipment (i.e., microscopes, teaching computers) that would be difficult to buy on their own.

Cottage *methodology* can also differ from traditional home schools. In some cottage groups, parents share the teaching responsibility, concentrating where possible on their subject strengths. Therefore, one couple may teach math, another history, another science, etc. These are known as subject co-ops and are growing in popularity. Or they may choose to teach all subjects and separate the children by general age groupings, one couple taking ages 7-10, another ages 11-13, etc. Still another possibility is for the cottage parents to hire a teacher, either from within its own parental midst or from outside it. Should a teacher be hired, it is very important for the parents to maintain a high level of involvement in the cottage education process. A parent hired from within will allow optimal control to remain in the hands of cottage parents. In a "paid" cottage school the teacher can devote full attention to teaching duties. Some of these may be mothers with previous teaching experience. As may be apparent, cottage education at this point begins to take on certain forms and characteristics of conventional private schooling.

Private Christian Schooling

If you feel uncomfortable with either the home or cottage schooling alternatives mentioned thus far, then conventional private education is your best choice. Private schooling successfully meets the educational needs of thousands upon thousands of American children and has a very important place in our democratic society. As articulated in earlier chapters, education belongs in the hands of parents. Education has always worked best when the government allows free market principles to operate. Learning flourishes in an environment when education is allowed to proceed unhindered by excessive government regulation and control. Chapter 3 reveals some of the negative learning consequences when the government sponsors, controls, and to a large extent monopolizes education. All schools that spring out of a free enterprise system should be warmly encouraged and allowed to flourish. Though some educrats fear it, healthy competition is the best solution for educational woes. That is why private schooling is the educational flower of a free enterprise society.

The comparison between public and private schools is like night and day. One parent with public school experience offers this unclouded advice to fellow parents: "Make whatever sacrifice you must, but keep your child *out* of the public school system. It would be better for you to live in a smaller house, to get by without that second car, to do without that boat or health club membership, than to send your child to a public school. If you treasure your child's spiritual, intellectual, and emotional future, do whatever it takes to keep him out of the public school system. Leaving your child in the public school should be an option of a last resort. Remember, damage done to your child in his early years can scar him for life." Why gamble with your child? The following conclusions were arrived at by two highly respected men who have researched and authored books on the subject of public education in America. Says Dr. Samuel Blumenfeld:

> There is only one way out for the American people. A massive exodus from the public schools into private ones where the freedom still exists to create a curriculum with a strong academic foundation.[1]

And Dr. Tim LaHaye gives Christian parents this advice:

> Unless you live in one of those rare school districts that rejects the stifling domination of humanists, as a Christian parent *you must first take your child out of the public school and send him to a Christian school.*[2] (emphasis mine)

Bureaucratic screaming for more funding in order to improve public education is a red herring. Even if more money is appropriated and spent, it is highly unlikely that genuine reform will move beyond the stage of political rhetoric. Why not put your child in a learning environment where he can come out on top? Consider the academic track record of private Christian schools.

> According to a 1983 study by the Association of Christian Schools International—which requires that member schools meet certain academic standards—students in ACSI schools scored significantly higher on a standardized achievement test than students in public schools at all grade levels. Eleventh-graders ranked sixteen months higher in terms of achievement than the national average.[3]

When choosing a private school, it is important to be conscientious and somewhat particular in your selection. Not all private schools are the same. Where possible, choose a private school that demonstrates at least the following qualities:

1) One that is distinctively Christian, and preferably evangelical in its philosophy and approach to education.

2) One that teaches the cardinal doctrines of Christianity without compromise (i.e., virgin birth, sinless life, death and resurrection of Jesus Christ, that Jesus is indeed the Son of God and the only Savior of mankind; that salvation by grace is available to all who have faith in His name).

3) One that teaches traditional values and respect for authority, domestic and otherwise.

4) One that reinforces the value of manners and etiquette.

5) One that encourages family life, and one that does not overemphasize homework to familial detriment.

6) One that does not overemphasize extracurricular activities which rob valuable family time.

7) One that has a low student/teacher ratio.

8) One that encourages parental involvement.

9) One that builds individuality and stimulates creativity.

10) One that teaches reading by phonics. Remember, reading is basic to all other learnable skills.

Above all, parents who choose private schooling for their children must remember to *retain the mantle of accountability*. Parents must not be tempted to ignore the God-ordained teaching process by surrendering both their authority and responsibility to surrogate parents—the private school teacher and staff. This is a departure from divine plan and order. In God's eyes, child training is considered the supreme duty of parents. It cannot be delegated. Parents do well to remember the distinction between *teaching* and *training*. The divine promise of Proverbs 22:6 is contingent upon *training* your child, not merely *teaching* him. Those who leave training up to the private schools will be sorely disappointed. The reason is simple; private schools are a *teaching* institution and not a *training* institution. Private schools function well in conjunction with parental *training*, but not in lieu of it. Moral and spiritual training is the parent's responsibility. Any attempt by parents to delegate that responsibility will result in failure. However, when private schools function as an extension of the home, they serve as a powerful education tool. This is when private Christian education is at its best. Because they are unfettered by government control, private schools retain an enormous amount of positive educational potential.

Why Home Schools and Private Schools Should Cooperate

Despite potential differences in approach and methodology, there must always remain a mutual respect and cooperation between private and home education. Neither private schools, cottage schools, or single-family home schools are an island to themselves. Each complements the other. Home schoolers should not smugly and narcissistically wave the pious flag of self-admiration over their accomplishments. Nor should private schools pejoratively look down their noses at home schoolers as though they were academically inferior and expendable. Both have their place and purpose in a free society.

Further, both have a common enemy. The Devil is not only the archenemy of God's Word, he is also the enemy of the free enterprise system that allows it to be taught openly in our private schools. The Bible says, "For our struggle is not against flesh and blood, but against the rulers, against the authorities, against the powers of this dark world and against the spiritual forces of evil in the heavenly realms" (Eph. 6:12). Our enemy is not merely a liberal political system or humanistic point of view. Our enemy is more formidable than that, and all private educators need to stand together against him with the full armor of God. The most important area of united activity should be in prayer. Both should mobilize their prayer warriors to pray that their educational rights and freedoms are not violated.

Another way to cooperate is legislatively. If either ignores or lets the other fall without rushing to aid them, they are cutting their own throat. For example, if home schoolers are outlawed by legislative statute or political manipulation in state education agencies, it will not be long before they go after conventional private schools. Government regulation and control, no matter how noble and ostensibly necessary its original purpose, has a voracious appetite that by nature grows uncurbed and with great rapidity. Such government control is similar to a camel who places his nose in a tent and simply will not be happy until he occupies the whole tent. A malicious attack has already been started on private schools. Says Dr. Tim LaHaye:

> Since 1979 the IRS has tried to lift the tax-deductible status of Christian schools if they did not establish racial quotas. . . . Big brother humanist, not satisfied with his dictatorial powers in the public sector, demands the right to run even our Christian schools.[4]

And Dr. Blumenfeld states:

> . . . The NEA is pressing for the regulation of private schools. Such regulations are already on the books of many states.[5]

Parental rights over your child are at stake. We are talking about fundamental constitutional rights here. We dare not let either one be bullied or harassed without defending their rights. What happens to one will eventually happen to the other. This is a sobering thought, but one which is undeniably true. Inherent in the fabric of a democratic society is the idea that children belong to their parents and are responsible for them. Parental authority involves making an educational choice for their children. Their choice may be to home teach or to delegate certain aspects of the educational process to a public or private school. Children do not belong to the state or an institution of the state. According to the United States Constitution, states are responsible for *supporting* the parent's role, not *supplanting* it. However, somewhere along the line it seems that philosophy has been turned around. Hence, both private and home schools must work together to help restore it.

Another area of cooperation might be for more private schools to serve as satellite headquarters for home schoolers. Using their existing staff, private schools could offer valuable oversight and experiential guidance for home educators. In addition, they could offer usage of their school facilities and participation in some of their campus activities (i.e., art classes, gymnasium and library usage, music, drama, field trips, sports, science fairs, standardized testing, etc.). In exchange, home educators could pay a nominal tuition, which when combined with other home schooling families could provide a welcome source of additional revenue. Further, upper-grade home schoolers are a potentially strong "feeder source" of pupils for Christian schools. And the students they enroll will be of a high caliber. Hence, cooperation between private and home schools is mutually beneficial.

A Final Thought

This book was written with the hope of showing parents three things: 1) why they should consider the home schooling alternative; 2) they are qualified to teach if they are a responsible, godly model, willing to count the cost involved and pay the price; and

3) how to get started in home schooling. However, if we have only succeeded in elucidating the precarious nature of public education, and have moved you to examine your educational alternatives, then we have accomplished our goal.

APPENDIX A

Common Questions Asked About Home Schooling

T hose who are seriously considering home schooling or who have recently begun to home school are usually besieged with a barrage of questions both from within and without. This appendix will briefly address and summarize twelve of the most commonly asked questions.

1) *Is it legal?* To answer this question in a word, "Yes." Hundreds of thousands of children all over America from kindergarten to twelfth grade are being home educated within the framework of the law. Many parents teach in complete freedom under the blessings of the law. Others comply to varying state regulations which govern the existence of a private school. A concise legal consideration of home schooling appears in a well-documented book coauthored by two attorneys. In summarizing their book they say:

> The constitutional right to employ home education is protected by numerous provisions of the United States Constitution, including freedom of religious exercise, freedom of speech and philosophic belief, the right to privacy, and the right to parental liberty. The state lacks any compelling interest in prohibiting or intrusively regulating home education. Moreover, the state has not used the least burdensome means of permitting home education.[1]

Now each state may stipulate conditional requirements for home schooling families to comply with. But home schoolers need not fear these requirements. In fact, some of them are written for their legal protection. School districts or states who challenge home schooling families frequently find themselves in for a real surprise. They often find that there is a problem with encroachment of constitutional rights based in the First, Ninth, and Fourteenth Amendments. Perhaps that is why "several states have recently deregulated and authorized home instruction, including Georgia, Montana, Mississippi, Colorado, Louisiana, and Arizona."[2] And more states are examining home education each year. The Hewitt Research Foundation in Washougal, Washington, recently reported that laws permitting home schooling have been passed in forty-two of fifty-five U.S. jurisdictions (the fifty states plus American Samoa, the District of Columbia, Guam, Puerto Rico, and the Virgin Islands).[3] Still, there are many uninformed people who love to create laws "in their minds" that simply do not exist. Then armed with these mental laws, they try to incite fear into the hearts of those who are law-abiding and conscientious.

Prudent home schoolers focus on their constitutionally-guaranteed rights rather than state-by-state laws which are continually being modified and revamped. They do not walk about in nervous fear wringing their hands over potential truancy charges or compulsory attendance laws. That would prove fruitless. They do stand up for their fundamental constitutional rights, which all U.S. citizens are guaranteed will be enforced unabatedly. Those few home schoolers who are challenged in court will do well to remember the Scripture which says: "After I looked things over, I stood up and said to the nobles, the officials and the rest of the people; 'Don't be afraid of them. Remember the Lord, who is great and awesome, and fight for your brothers, your sons, your daughters, your wives and your homes'" (Neh. 4:14).

For those who desire to study further their constitutional rights in the matter, I recommend the book *Home Education and Constitutional Liberties*, published by Crossway Books.

2) *Will my child miss out on socialization?* No, emphatically not! As we mentioned in Chapter 4, there are two types of socialization, positive and negative. Positive sociability is best summarized as that which builds responsibility, cooperation, kindness, fidelity, love, and bilateral trust. It molds a good self-image which delights in putting others first. Negative sociability, on the other hand, involves age-segregation, criticism and derision, rivalry, contention, unhealthy judgment and evaluation by peers, social withdrawal, and selfishness. It molds a poor self-esteem which responds quickly to peer pressure, creating the unfortunate tendency toward peer-dependency.

Many parents have been convinced that small children need

to be around others their own age to be socialized. This dangerous educational myth leads well-intentioned parents to false assumptions. So powerful is this strange notion that many parents might concede to the viability of academic instruction at home, but will still insist on the need for regular group interaction in order to develop and master their social skills. Most believe that conventional schools provide the best environment for meeting this assumed socialization requirement. Sound research, however, lends little credibility to this convenient sentiment.

Without a doubt, a loving, outreaching home environment is the best socializer a young child could possibly have. A home schooled child tends to mix freely with all ages and not just a narrow age grouping. This can become problematic for children schooled in mass education, especially in the older ages.

A young child learns good sociability primarily by watching and mirroring. Do you want your child to model after you or after his peers, after his teachers at school or his teachers at home? But the bottom line is this: what kind of socialization do you want, positive or negative? After you have decided this, the overwhelming evidence will quickly unveil where each kind is bred and nurtured.

3) *Do I have the qualifications to teach?* You do if you qualify as a genuinely concerned and loving parent. Many home educators have nothing more than a high school diploma and a desire to teach their own, and yet they have experienced a teaching success that is enviable. Based on the dismal record of the public school system, I certainly wouldn't tout teaching degrees and certification as either an asset or a qualification. However, the academic track record of home schoolers is certainly worthy of public aggrandizement.

In 1837, the Massachusetts State Senate began the first statewide system of public education in the United States. However, it wasn't until about the mid-1870s that teaching took on the appearance of an accepted profession. Hence, teaching as a vocation is a relatively recent phenomenon. In spite of widespread teacher training and certification, contemporary public education has had questionable effectiveness. Not only have academic test scores fallen miserably in the past twenty years, but youngsters have also been left meandering in moral aimlessness. Does this seem like quality education to you?

A brief Biblical explanation of the teaching process would be helpful here. The Bible uses several key words for teaching and training. One of these words is the Hebrew *chanak*, which means "to train, dedicate, or make narrow." This word occurs five times in the Bible: Deuteronomy 20:5 (two times), 1 Kings 8:63, 2 Chronicles 7:5, Proverbs 22:6. The ancient root of this word means "to make narrow" or "to strangle." Applied to the teaching process, it implies that parents are to restrict the path their children may take. The Bible teaches that parents are responsible for getting their child started in the right direction. A child must not be allowed to go whatever course or direction he so chooses. Contrary to the leading of his old nature, parents are to set him on the right course and help him remain there. His path must be restricted or narrowed, for " . . . Narrow the road that leads to life, and only a few find it" (Matt. 7:14).[4]

Proverbs 22:6 says, "Train (*chanak*) a child in the way he should go, and when he is old he will not turn from it." The common usage of the word *chanak* implies dedication of a building or child (cf. references above). The Old Testament rite of dedicating the Temple is analogous to the dedication of a child, especially in the fact that both are done when they are new or young. The only comparative difference is that for a child, dedicating and training is not a one-time initiation but a continual childhood process.[5]

Another Biblical word for the teaching process is *shanan*, which means "to sharpen, to inculcate, to teach by repetition." Godly values and standards are taught best when children are inculcated with the Word of God repetitiously throughout the day. Deuteronomy 6:6, 7 clearly gives this responsibility to parents: "These commandments that I give you today are to be upon your hearts. Impress them on your children. Talk about them when you sit at home and when you walk along the road, when you lie down and when you get up." The holy writer clearly intends for godly teaching and training to take place daily, utilizing every opportunity. Obviously, Christian truths are to be repeated continually until the child begins to walk in the way of God on his own.[6]

Yet another Biblical word for the teaching process is the word *lamad*, which means "to teach by intensive drill" (cf. Deut. 4:10 and 11:9). *Lamad* is used to describe the goading of cattle (Hosea 10:11), and the training of military recruits (1 Chron. 5:18). A goad is a sharp stick used to penetrate animal hide to prod and thus direct cattle. Children sometimes need to be figuratively prodded to keep them moving in a godly direction. Soldiers are trained intensively that they might be prepared for the potential threat of warfare. We know that every Christian is subject to intense spiritual warfare from demonic origin. Hence a child must be taught intensively how to deal with it, like a soldier preparing for battle.[7]

Implicit in Biblical thought is the idea that teaching authority has been divinely given to the parents. That is where it properly belongs. Like the charge given to the apostles to "... present everyone perfect in Christ" (Col. 1:28), parents are charged with a similar training responsibility for their children and are held accountable for the end result. No one can adequately fill the shoes of this great responsibility quite like parents. To reach maximum effectiveness, proper teaching of God's truth requires 1) daily inculcation, 2) life application, 3) parental modeling, and 4) merging with all other disciplines. Who better than parents can fulfill these qualifications?

This is not to say that parents are an educational island unto themselves, teaching and imparting knowledge apart from any social context whatsoever. Parents must also view their teaching and training responsibilities as a citizen in their local community and, more importantly, as a part of the body of Christ. It is to be remembered that home schooling is an educational endeavor centered around the home, but extends outside of it as well.

Parental tutoring is the Biblical ideal for the education of children. Children are accountable to their parents who in turn are accountable to God. Mass education is at best a substitute for the principal educators, the parents. Since classroom schooling has held sway for over a century in America, many parents have forgotten who is held responsible for their child's development. No school, public or private, can ever hope to do a better job of developing character and values quite like loving and devoted Christian parents. What kind of values can be taught a child in a public school where teachers must remain instructionally "amoral"? Not only is their certification label of questionable value, but they also lack the qualifications for being the primary instructors of Biblical truth upon which all knowledge is hinged. It must also be remembered that sending a child off to parochial school does not exempt parents from the divine charge in Deuteronomy 6 and Ephesians 6:1. Parochial schools will never hold the educational qualifications of responsible, Christian parents when it comes to the teaching and mirroring of spiritual truth.

This is not meant to be a slam against teachers, but a defense of loving home educators, the most honorable mentors the world has ever known. There are two basic qualifications for

Christian home educators. First, they need to develop, nurture, and exhibit a godly example. Second, they must sit down and seriously count the cost (Luke 14:28, 29) and be willing to pay the price. Though they can choose to delegate their teaching responsibilities, the divine charge firmly rests upon parents. You do not need a teaching degree or certificate to qualify as a good teacher. You do need a loving concern for the overall development of your child's well-being (academic, moral, self-image, social, physical, and spiritual), simultaneously following a few simple educational guidelines. Parents willing to meet the above requirements are indeed qualified.

4) *Are home schooled children accepted in college and accredited schools?* Yes! Most schools judge a child's academic competence based on his performance on standardized testing instruments. With home schoolers scoring 80 percent on such tests, 30 percentile above the average classroom child, it is doubtful they will be denied entrance into the finer institutions of learning. If past history is representative of the future, home schoolers will continue to be prime admission targets of universities and colleges. Many home instructors test their child regularly to know where he stands in relation to his peers at any given time. Hence, there are usually few surprises.

5) *Will my child miss out on extracurricular activities?* Not at all! If anything, he will enjoy more. In metropolitan areas, local home schooling families frequently join together to enjoy extracurricular activities. Here are a few of the things they can do and learn:

1) Visit the county courthouse—learn about justice and law.

2) Visit historical sites—learn about historical America.

3) Attend cultural events—learn culture through art, plays, ballets.

4) Attend sports events—learn about recreation/sports.

5) Visit manufacturing plants—learn about how goods /products are made.

6) Visit police/fire departments—learn about how crime /fires are fought.

7) Visit public libraries—check out books, learn about library services.

8) Visit ranches and farms—learn how we get milk, butter, eggs, meat, etc. Also learn about animals & nature.

9) Visit airport/train station—learn about transportation.

10) Visit T.V./newspaper office—learn about how news is communicated.

These are but a few of the many extracurricular activities home schooling families engage in. Since these activities are often done as a family, they are a great deal more pleasurable. This in turn creates a better learning environment for your child.

6) *At what age should I begin?* It is very important to remember that learning readiness is not schooling readiness. Most children have a decided interest in learning from birth on. Many parents confuse an interest in learning with preparedness to start school. This is an unfortunate assumption. Children may be able to learn basic concepts, facts, and ideas without being able to emotionally handle the demands and methods that are placed on them in a mass educational setting. Many children are not ready for formal academic instruction until they reach the age of about eight or ten. The key is not to do too much too early. That is the regrettable mistake of the education system right now. Take it easy! Enjoy your child and let him enjoy you. In the early years concentrate on character development.

7) *How advanced of a grade should I teach to?* From a spiritual perspective, parents should have the goal of teaching until their child has demonstrated the self-evident maturity of being the salt and light of the world. By this we mean developing the ability for your child to resist the strong peer-dependent tendencies inherent in mass education. We mean the ability to walk in the ways of God, firmly standing on Biblical convictions in the face of social opposition and worldly enticements. Such abilities come with age maturity and godly role modeling.

Beyond this, endeavor to teach as long as you feel comfortable, remembering to undertake the challenge a year at a time. There is no set rule or standard. Remember, even a few years of home education is better than none. Many home schooled children show marked elevation over their peers with just a couple of years of home tutoring. Some parents have the goal of teaching through sixth grade, some through junior high, and still others all the way through high school. Teach them as long as you can comfortably accomplish your spiritual and educational goals.

However, parents must be careful not to focus on their abilities and inabilities. To do so bases your answer to the above question on your feelings rather than on your child's need.

8) *How many children can I teach at home?* As many as you have. One family in New Mexico enjoys home schooling their children—all *ten* of them. And with great success, I might add. The mother has nothing more than a high school diploma and home schools children with an age span from two to fourteen. The two oldest children, Alexandra (age fourteen) and Christopher (thirteen), are completing academic work at a major university in the U.S. Their younger sister, Francesca (twelve), just started classes at the same university. The child next in line, Dominic (eleven), should gradate from high school this year. All the rest are excelling academically at a remarkable rate. The parents have no outside help with either teaching or housework, and yet still manage to run a profitable thoroughbred horse ranch. The inference is obvious. Responsible and loving parents can successfully and competently teach all of their children, even if they have ten.

9) *Will I have the time to teach?* Remember, you do not need to teach your child for six or seven hours a day! Not even conventional schools do that. Recent research shows that students are exposed to about two hours of "teacher talk" during a five-period day. And out of that, an average of seven minutes a day involves teachers' responses to individual students.[8] It doesn't take much for home educators to exceed that unfortunate amount of one-on-one communication. The consistency of private tutoring allows most home educators to accomplish an incredible amount of teaching in two to three hours a day. With that, most are easily able to supersede a conventional school in quality academic instruction.

Potential home schoolers sometimes fear that they will lose the freedom and time to do the things they enjoy. But properly structured, home schooling will not rob you of time with your spouse, friends, or time to just be by yourself. It can even enhance these times and make them more meaningful. With just a little organization, home schooling is within the grasp of every concerned and loving parent.

Home schooling does require a commitment on the part of the parents. Part of that commitment requires an assessment of priorities. When you boil it all down, what are the most important things in life? Your career? Your house? Your hobbies? Your financial assets? Your personal entertainment? Or your child?

Each needs to be placed in its proper perspective. Your child is with you but for a few short years and then he is gone. The time you have to spend with your child is precious and numbered. Parents who are willing to commit themselves to the process will find home schooling both rewarding and within reach.

10) *Will my child listen to me and accept me as his teacher?* If your child listens and responds to your parental authority now, he will have little problem accepting you as an academic teacher at home. However, if you have less respect and control over your child than you would like to have, the home school environment will be your best opportunity to regain it. We have examined the ill-effects of conventional classroom schooling and have seen that rebellion against parental authority is frequently a result. Peer dependency and growing antifamily attitudes in educational circles is believed to be eroding this traditional respect. However, as a home educator, you can reclaim and nurture this vital attribute. In sum, if child-parent responsiveness is important to you, home education is probably your best avenue for promoting it.

11) *Should I defend my decision to home school before friends and family?* From time to time one might be challenged or criticized for their decision to home school. Depending on who it is and the importance of your relationship, you may want to explain your reasons. This may be true in the case of immediate family and close friends. However, be very careful to what degree you defend your decision. Remember that your primary accountability belongs to God.

Some criticize out of ignorance, others out of plain jealousy. Those who criticize out of ignorance sometimes show understanding when false reasoning is exposed. Those who criticize out of jealousy do so because they are defending their own erroneous excuses. Here are a few common excuses people give for not home schooling:

1) My child's teacher is the exception, she/he is excellent.

2) We are in a good school district.

3) My child loves school.

4) My child doesn't seem to be having any problems.

5) My child needs the socialization that comes with a school.

6) I don't have the time to teach my child at home.

7) I don't have room in my house to teach.

8) I am not organized enough to home school.

9) It's just not for me.

10) I don't think home schooling is legal.

11) I send my child to a private school.

12) My child would not obey me.

13) I need my time alone.

14) Public schools aren't all that bad.

15) My child needs the extracurricular activities that public school offers.

16) I'm not qualified.

17) I believe in being taught by certified teachers.

18) I believe a child needs competition to help him learn.

It is important for parents to know why they home school, but it is not important for them to spend all their time defending that decision to others. As you can see, there are many excuses people give for not home schooling. To satisfy their own lack of action, they will attempt to thrust these excuses onto you. Some may have an element of validity, many do not. It hurts when parents and friends do not understand and lend support, but don't expect them to. If everyone understood, we wouldn't have our current education crisis.

Some merely need to have home education logically explained to them. In that case, share whatever information or books that helped you make your decision, like this one. Others with closed minds will never budge and will argue for the sake of arguing. The book of Proverbs gives this advice: "Do not speak to a fool, for he will scorn the wisdom of your words" (Proverbs 23:9). In short, know your reasons, explain them to those to whom you feel it necessary, but don't feel compelled to advertise your decision and defend it to every acquaintance.

12) *What curriculum should I use?* Common sense, veteran advice, research, and a little experience will give you the best guidance in choosing curriculum that is right for you. Under the "research" area, it is helpful to attend home school curriculum fairs and workshops, as well as placing your name on mailing

lists of various curriculum publishers. An excellent resource guide in this area is Mary Pride's book *The Big Book of Home Learning*. There are many excellent publishers of home school curriculum. When selecting from the top contenders, it would be difficult to make a major mistake in curriculum. Some parents choose to teach exclusively from one publishing house. Others choose publishers whom they feel excel in a given subject, using for example, one publisher for math, one for penmanship, one for reading, etc.

Parents in local home schooling support groups will gladly give you curriculum suggestions based on their teaching experience. It is smart to listen to the advice of veteran home schoolers. At the same time, realize that there is no one curriculum that is right for every family. What may work well for them may not work well for you. As a general rule, it is wise for new home instructors to use a structured curriculum that correlates the various subjects and disciplines. At the same time, it is unwise to become bogged down in curriculum selection, since it is more critical to home school with the proper motives, attitudes, and goals. Good textbooks are important, but love, kindness, and consistency are more important. Academics have great worth, but stressing values, character, and spiritual development have more.

One would be remiss if he did not at least mention the "principle approach." Though it is not a specific curriculum per se, one can be developed from using it. The principle approach is a Biblical way of developing a world view based on God's Word. The approach is enhanced through the use of three things: a personal notebook, Webster's 1828 dictionary, and the Bible, The principle approach incorporates the following four steps: *researching, reasoning, relating, and recording*. Students research a subject using a dictionary and a Bible concordance, to see how the Scriptures approach and handle it. Then using their reason they discover the use of Biblical principles involved. Next they relate the Biblical principles to other students, character development, and self-government. Finally the student makes a written record of the process and any applications in a personal notebook.

The idea is to help students develop godly character while simultaneously mastering skills in various subject matter. They learn not only to grasp intellectual facts, but also to think through, analyze (in light of God's Word), and articulate their thoughts accordingly. There are *seven principles* which serve as the foundation for thought (hence, the name "principle approach"). They are:

1) God's principle of *individuality*.
2) The Christian principle of *self-government*.
3) America's heritage of *Christian character* which includes:
   a) Faith and steadfastness.
   b) Brotherly love and Christian care.
   c) Diligence and industry.
   d) Liberty and conscience.
4) *Conscience* is the *most sacred of all property*.
5) *The Christian form* of our *government*.
6) How the *seed* of local *self-government* is *planted*.
7) The Christian principle of *American political union*.[9]

Though not a curriculum, home schoolers would do well to acquaint themselves with the principle approach. For further information you can contact either of the following:

Foundation for American Christian Education
Box 27035
San Francisco, CA 94127

American Christian History Institute
1093 Beechwood Street
Camarillo, CA 93010

APPENDIX B

Recommendations

Recommended Magazines and Newsletters for Home Educators

1) *The Parent Educator and Family Report,* published by Hewitt Research Foundation, P.O. Box 9, Washougal, WA 98671-0009. (206) 835-8708
2) *The Teaching Home,* 8731 Everett Street, Portland, OR 97220. (503) 253-9633

Recommended Magazines for Children

1) *Bread for Children,* P.O. Box 1017, Arcadia, Florida, 33821.
2) *Evangelizing Today's Child,* Box 348, Warrenton, Missouri 63383

3) *Family Life Today*, 2300 Knoll Drive, Ventura, California 93003.

4) *God's Rainbows*, School of Education-O.R.U., 7777 S. Lewis, Tulsa, Oklahoma 74171.

Home School Legal Assistance Organizations

1) Home School Legal Defense Association, P.O. Box 2091, Washington, D.C. 20013. (202) 737-0030

2) National Association for the Legal Support of Alternate Schools, P.O. Box 2823, Santa Fe, New Mexico 87501. (505) 471-6928

Home School Research Organizations

1) Hewitt Research Foundation, P.O. Box 9, Washougal, Washington 98671-0009. (206) 835-8708 (Fine, well-established organization that stays abreast of current laws, latest scientific and educational data, and the growth of the home school movement in general.)

Recommended Curriculum for Character Education

1) *Character Foundation Curriculum*, published by the Association of Christian Schools International, P.O. Box 4097, Whittier, California, 90607. (213) 694-4791 (Excellent material which can be used in conjunction with most curriculums. Also recommended are the character flash cards that accompany this curriculum).

2) *Konos Character Curriculum*, Konos Inc., P.O. Box 1534, Richardson, TX 75083, (214) 669-8337.

3) *Character sketches*, Institute in Basic Youth Conflicts, Inc., Box One, Oak Brook, IL 60521. (Though not specifically designed as a curriculum, it can serve as excellent resource material. I.B.Y.C. also has a family game entitled *Character Cues*.)

Recommended Curriculum for Bible Instruction

1) *Radiant Christian School Bible Curriculum*, published by Gospel Publishing House, 1445 Boonville Avenue, Springfield, Missouri 65802. (417) 862-2781 (Excellent material; designed for grades 1-8.)

2) *Bible for Christian Schools*, published by Bob Jones University Press, Greenville, South Carolina 29614. (800) 845-5731 (Bible curriculum K-12.)

Recommended Curriculum for Manners and Etiquette

1) *Christian Charm* (for girls) and *Man in Demand* (for boys), published by Manna Publications, P.O. Box 1111, Camas, Washington 98607. (206) 834-3148

Recommended Curriculum for Reading and Writing

1) *Sing, Spell, Read & Write*, CBNU Extended University, Virginia Beach, VA 23463 (800) 446-READ. (This is an excellent curriculum for teaching children the fundamental skills of reading and writing. Best of all, the learning is made enjoyable.)
2) *The Writing Road to Reading*, Quill, 105 Madison Avenue, New York, NY 10016.

Notes

Chapter 1: Home Schooling: The Return of a Biblical Model of Education

1. Raymond and Dorothy Moore, *Home-Style Teaching* (Waco, Tex.: Word Books, 1984), p. 201.
2. Letter to the Secretary, Dept. of Education, from Dr. Raymond Moore, April 18, 1985, p. 1.
3. Bill Gothard, *Be Alert for Spiritual Danger* (Oak Brook, Ill.: Institute in Basic Youth Conflicts, 1980), p. 15.
4. Urie Bronfenbrenner and Maureen A. Mahoney, *Influences of Human Development* (Hinsdale, Ill.: Dryden Press, 1975), pp. 497-499.

Chapter 2: Is Home Schooling for You?

1. "Excellence and Opportunity: A Program of Support for American Education," *Phi Delta Kappan*, Sept. 1984, p. 15.
2. "The 16th Annual Gallup Poll of the Public's Attitudes Toward the Public Schools," *Phi Delta Kappan*, Sept. 1984, p. 25.
3. Mel and Norma Gabler, *What Are They Teaching Our Children?* (Wheaton, Ill.: Victor Books, 1985), p. 88.

4. Paul C. Vitz, *Censorship: Evidence of Bias in Our Children's Textbooks* (Ann Arbor, Mich.: Servant, 1986), n.p.

5. Stanley Coopersmith, *The Antecedents of Self-Esteem*, (San Francisco: Freeman and Company, 1967), pp. 164-166.

6. Raymond and Dorothy Moore, *Home Grown Kids* (Waco, Tex.: Word Books, 1981), p. 39.

7. "A Study of Schooling: Some Findings and Hypotheses," *Phi Delta Kappan*, March 1983.

8. Raymond and Dorothy Moore, *Home Style Teaching* (Waco, Tex.: Word Books, 1984), p. 156.

9. Raymond and Dorothy Moore, *Home Grown Kids*, pp. 32-33.

10. David Elkind, *The Hurried Child* (Reading, Mass.: Addison-Wesley Publishing Company, 1981), p. 157.

11. *United States Supreme Court Reports: Lawyers' Edition*, Second Series (Rochester: Lawyers Co-operative Publishing Co., 1973), p. 35.

12. William J. Bennett, *First Lessons: A Report on Elementary Education in America* (Washington, D.C.: U.S. Government Printing Office: 1986), p. 10.

Chapter 3: Public Education: The Assault on Excellence

1. Tim LaHaye, *The Battle for the Public Schools* (Old Tappan, N.J.: Fleming Revell, 1983), p. 13.

2. Jonathan Kozol, *Illiterate America* (Garden City, N.Y.: Anchor Press/Doubleday, 1985), pp. 8, 9.

3. "Factors Associated with Test Score Decline," briefing paper prepared for the U.S. Dept. of Education—National Center for Education Statistics, December, 1984, p. 1.

4. Jonathan Kozol, *Illiterate America*, p. 16.

5. *Ibid.*, p. 18.

6. "16th Annual Gallup Poll of Public's Attitudes Toward the Public Schools," *Phi Delta Kappan*, Sept. 1984, p. 24.

7. Jonathan Kozol, *Illiterate America*, p. 5.

8. Phyllis Schlafly, *Child Abuse in the Classroom* (Alton, Ill.: Pere Marquette Press, 1984), p. 13.

9. 5 May 1983, *Congressional Record*, S6060.

10. "Another Study Says Schools Are in Peril," *Washington Post*, 21 July 1983.

11. Sally Reed, *NEA: Propaganda Front of the Radical Left* (Alexandria, Va.: NCBE, 1984), p. 25.

12. *Ibid.*

13. "Johnny Can't Count—the Dangers for the U.S.," *U.S. News and World Report*, 15 September 1982, p. 46.

14. "A New Test Begins for America's Schools," *U.S. News and World Report*, 9 September 1985, p. 63.

15. William J. Bennett, *First Lessons: A Report on Elementary Education in America* (Washington, D.C.: Government Printing Office, 1986), p. 24.
16. *Ibid.*, p. 26.
17. "Help! Teacher Can't Teach!," *Time*, 16 June 1980, pp. 55, 57, 58.
18. Samuel L. Blumenfeld, *NEA: Trojan Horse in American Education* (Boise, Idaho: Paradigm Company, 1984), p. 211.
19. *Ibid.*, pp. 57, 58.
20. Tim LaHaye, *The Battle for the Public School*, p. 14.
21. Mel and Norma Gabler, *What Are They Teaching Our Children?* (Wheaton, Ill.: Victor Books, 1985), p. 20.
22. Paul Copperman, *The Literacy Hoax* (New York: William Morrow and Company, 1978), p. 79.
23. Mel and Norma Gabler, *What Are They Teaching Our Children?*, p. 56.
24. William J. Bennett, *First Lessons: A Report on Elementary Education in America*, p. 22.
25. Samuel L. Blumenfeld, *Trojan Horse in American Education*, p. 103.
26. "Mastery Learning: Tool of Totalitarians," *The Barbara M. Morris Report*, 29, September/October 1985, p. 1.
27. *Ibid.*, p. 1.
28. Charlotte T. Iserbyt, *Back to Basics or . . . Skinnerian International Curriculum?* (Upland: Barbara Morris Report, 1985), pp. 12, 13.
29. William J. Bennett, *First Lessons: A Report on Elementary Education in America*, p. 62.
30. Gabler, *What Are They Teaching Our Children?*, p. 54.
31. *Ibid.*, p. 53.
32. David L. Bender, *American Values*, 2nd ed. (St. Paul, Minn.: Greenhaven Press, 1984), p. 172.
33. Verne Faust, *Self-Esteem in the Classroom* (San Diego, Caif.: Thomas Paine Press, 1980), p. 258.
34. "Help! Teacher Can't Teach!," *Time*, 16 June 1980, p. 54.
35. Paul Copperman, *The Literacy Hoax* (New York: William Morrow and Company, 1978), p. 103.
36. Paul A. Kienel, "The Academic and Moral Decline of Public Education: A Major Threat to the Church," *Christian School Comment*, p. 1.
37. "The Valedictorian," *Newsweek*, 6 Sept. 1976, p. 52.
38. Paul Copperman, *The Literacy Hoax*, pp. 103-105.
39. *Ibid.*, p. 106.
40. Tim LaHaye, *The Battle for the Public Schools*, p. 26.
41. "Help! Teacher Can't Teach," *Time*, 16 June 1980, p. 55.

42. Paul C. Vitz, et. al., "Religion and Traditional Values in Public School Textbooks: An Empirical Study," (study pursuant to a grant contract from the National Institute of Education, Department of Education), pp. 70, 71.

43. "Secular Humanism in the Dock," *Newsweek*, 27 October 1986, p. 96.

44. *Ibid.*, p. 96.

45. Phyllis Schlafly, *Child Abuse in the Classroom*, p. 85.

46. *Ibid.*, p. 312.

47. *Dolan Report Newsletter*, 1, No. 5, June 1985 p. 1.

48. Mel and Norma Gabler, *What Are They Teaching Our Children?*, p. 66.

49. *Ibid.*, p. 66.

50. *Surgeon General's Report on Acquired Immune Deficiency Syndrome*, p. 31.

51. *Ibid.*, pp. 31, 32.

52. Barrett Mosbacker, *Teen Pregnancy and School-based Health Clinics* (Washington, D.C.: Family Research Council of America, Inc.), p. 1.

53. House Select Committee on Children, Youth and Families, *Teen Pregnancy: What Is Being Done? A State-by-state Look*, December 1985, p. 378.

54. *Family Planning Perspectives*, 12, No. 5, September/October 1980, p. 229.

55. Barrett Mosbacker, *Teen Pregnancy and School-based Health Clinics*, p. 6.

56. *Schools Without Drugs* (Washington, D.C.: U.S. Department of Education, 1986), p. 5.

57. *Ibid.*

58. *Ibid.*

59. *Ibid.*, p. 8.

60. *Ibid.*, p. iv.

61. Verne Faust, *Self-esteem in the Classroom*, p. 41.

62. Mel and Norma Gabler, *What Are They Teaching Our Children?*, p. 101.

63. *Ibid.*, p. 86.

64. *Ibid.*

65. Tim LaHaye, *The Battle for the Public Schools*, p. 197.

66. *Ibid.*, pp. 179, 180.

67. Mel and Norma Gabler, *What Are They Teaching Our Children?*, p. 101.

68. *Ibid.*, p. 102.

69. Phyllis Schlafly, *Child Abuse in the Classroom*, pp. 368, 371.

70. *Ibid.*, p. 90.

71. Verne Faust, *Self-esteem in the Classroom*, p. 40.
72. *Ibid.*, p. 42.
73. *Ibid.*, p. 38.
74. *Ibid.*, p. 60.
75. "Teaching Children the Facts of Life and Death: Suicide Prevention in the Schools," Charlotte P. Ross.
76. Verne Faust, *Self-esteem in the Classroom*, p. 38.
77. James Dobson, *How to Build Self-esteem in Your child* (Old Tappan, N.J.: Fleming Revell, 1979), p. 62.
78. *Ibid.*, pp. 47, 48.
79. *Ibid.*, p. 63.
80. Verne Faust, *Self-esteem in the Classroom*, p. 40.
81. "16th Annual Gallup Poll of the Public's Attitudes Towards the Public School," *Phi Delta Kappan*, Sept. 1984, p. 25.
82. "Restoring Order to the Public Schools," *Phi Delta Kappan*, March 1985, p. 490.
83. David Elkind, *The Hurried Child* (Reading, Mass.: Addison-Wesley Publishing Co., 1981), p. 155.
84. *Survey of NEA K-12 Teacher Members 1985* (National Education Association, Professional and Organizational Development/Research Division: 1985), p. 18.
85. "Most Teachers in Poll Cite Low Pay, Consider Quitting," *Fort Worth Star-Telegram*, 12 Nov. 1986.
86. "Restoring Order to the Public Schools," *Phi Delta Kappan*, March 1985, p. 490.
87. "Japanese Schools: There Is Much We Can Learn," *U.S. News and World Report*, 2 Sept. 1985, p. 43.
88. Mel and Norma Gabler, *What Are They Teaching Our Children?*, pp. 21, 22.
89. Emily Post, *The New Emily Post's Etiquette* (The Emily Post Institute, Inc., 1975), p. preface.
90. Phyllis Schlafly, *Child Abuse in the Classroom*, p. 113.
91. Mel and Norma Gabler, *What Are They Teaching Our Children?*, p. 60.
92. *Ibid.*, p. 57.
93. Tim La Haye, *The Battle for the Public Schools*, p. 13.
94. Phyllis Schlafly, *Child Abuse in the Classroom*, p. 21.
95. Samuel L. Blumenfeld, *NEA: Trojan Horse in American Education*.
96. "U.S. Teachers Held Hostage by the N.E.A.," *Human Events*, 7 Sept. 1985, p. 12.
97. *Ibid.*, p. 14.
98. "A Religion for a New Age," *The Humanist*, Jan/Feb. 1983.

Chapter 4: Why Home Schooling Is the Best Alternative

1. "Growing Without Schooling," *Radcliffe Quarterly*, March 1978, p. 9.
2. Raymond S. Moore, "Research and Common Sense: Therapies for our Homes and Schools," *Teachers College Record*, 84, No. 2 (Winter 1982), p. 365.
3. John Bowlby, *Deprivation of Maternal Care* (New York: Schocken Books, 1966), p. 68.
4. John Holt, *Teach Your Own* (New York: Delacorte Press, 1981), p. 51.
5. Raymond and Dorothy Moore, *Home-spun Schools* (Waco, Tex.: Word Books, 1982), pp. 10, 11.
6. Quote from Holt, *Teach Your Own*, pp. 51-53.
7. Raymond and Dorothy Moore, *Home-spun Schools*, pp. 10, 11.
8. "Home Schooling: Up from the Underground," *Reason Magazine*, April 1983, p. 25.
9. "Home Schooling: An Idea Whose Time has Returned," *Human Events*, 15 Sept. 1984.
10. "The School at Home," *Moody Monthly*, March 1984, pp. 18, 19.
11. *Ibid.*, p. 19.
12. *Ibid.*
13. "Home Schooling: Up from the Underground," *Reason Magazine*, pp. 23, 24.
14. *Ibid.*, p. 27.
15. *Webster's New Collegiate Dictionary* (Springfield, Mass.: G. & C. Merriam Co., 1973), p. 748.
16. Particia H. Berne and Louis M. Savary, *Building Self-esteem in Children* (New York: Continuum Publishing Co., 1981), p. xv.
17. Janet Kizziar and Judy Hagedorn, *Search for Acceptance: The Adolescent and Self-esteem* (Chicago: Nelson-Hall, 1979), p. 2.
18. Dorothy C. Briggs, *Your Child's Self-esteem: The Key to Life* (Garden City, N.Y.: Doubleday, 1970), p. 20.
19. "Home Schooling: An Idea Whose Time has Returned," *Human Events*.
20. James Dobson, *Hide and Seek*, (Old Tappan, N.J.: Fleming Revell, 1974), p. 75.
21. Shirley C. Samuels, *Enhancing Self-concept in Early Childhood* (New York: Human Science Press: 1977), p. 34.
22. "Research and Common Sense: Therapies for our Homes and Schools," *Teachers College Record* Winter 1982, p. 366.

23. John Bowlby, *Deprivation of Maternal Care*, pp. 15-29.
24. James Dobson, *Hide and Seek*, p. 80.
25. *Ibid.*, p. 38.
26. Robert H. Schuller, *Self-esteem: The New Reformation* (Waco, Tex.: Word Books, 1982), p. 17.
27. "Home Schooling: Up from the Underground," *Reason Magazine*, April 1983, p. 26.
28. "New Research on Sociability," *The Parent Educator and Family Report*, 4, No. 3 (May/June 1986), p. 1.
29. Verne Faust, *Self-esteem in the Classroom*, p. 61.
30. Nathan Pritikin, *The Pritikin Promise* (New York: Pocket Books, 1983), p. 10.
31. "Why Parents Should Enroll their Children in a Christian School," *Christian School Comment*, 15, No. 6.
32. Mel and Norma Gabler, *What Are They Teaching Our children?* (Wheaton, Ill.: Victor Books, 1985), p. 34.
33. "The Gallup Poll of Teacher's Attitudes Toward the Public Schools," *Phi Delta Kappan*, Oct. 1984, p. 101.
34. *United States Supreme Court Reports: Lawyer's Edition*, Second Series (Rochester: Lawyer's Co-operative Publishing Co., 1973), p. 24.
35. Raymond and Dorothy Moore, "Research and Common Sense: Therapies for our Homes and Schools," *Teachers College Record*, 84, No. 2 (Winter 1982), p. 372.
36. Urie Bronfenbrenner and Maureen A. Mahoney, *Influences of Human Development* (Hinsdale, Ill.: Dryden Press, 1975), p. 491.
37. Raymond and Dorothy Moore, *Home-Grown Kids* (Waco, Tex.: Word Books, 1981), pp. 37, 38.
38. *Ibid.*, p. 23.
39. *Ibid.*, p. 26.
40. Raymond and Dorothy Moore, *Home-style Teaching* (Waco, Tex.: Word Books, 1984), pp. 36, 37.

Chapter 6: How to Begin

1. Philip May, *Which Way to Educate* (Chicago: Moody Press, 1975), pp. 96-98.
2. Allan C. Carlson, "What Happened to the Family Wage?", *The Public Interest*, 83 (Spring 1986), p. 13.
3. *Ibid.*, p. 13.
4. H. W. Byrne, *A Christian Approach to Education* (Grand Rapids: Zondervan Publishing House, 1961), pp. 97-99.
5. *Ibid.*, p. 101.
6. *Ibid.*, p. 101.

Chapter 8: Choosing Other Private Education Alternatives

1. Samuel L. Blumenfeld, *NEA: Trojan Horse in American Education*, (Boise, Idaho: The Paradigm Company, 1984), p. 247.
2. Tim LaHaye, *The Battle for the Public Schools* (Old Tappan, N.J.: Fleming H. Revell Company, 1983), p. 252.
3. Mel and Norma Gabler, *What Are They Teaching Our Children?* (Wheaton, Ill.: Victor Books, 1985), p. 180.
4. LaHaye, *The Battle for the Public Schools,* pp. 254, 255.
5. Samuel L. Blumenfeld, *NEA: Trojan Horse in American Education*, p. 247.

Appendix A: Common Questions Asked About Home Schooling

1. John Whitehead and Wendell Bird, *Home Education and Constitutional Liberties* (Westchester, Ill.: Crossway Books, 1984), p. 117.
2. *Ibid.*, p. 80.
3. "Home-schooled Children Score Above Average on Tests," *Focus on the Family*, January 1986, p. 10.
4. J. Richard Fugate, *What the Bible Says About . . . Child Training* (Garland, Tex.: Aletheia Publishers, Inc., 1980), pp. 65-69.
5. *Ibid.*, pp. 65-69.
6. *Ibid.*
7. *Ibid.*
8. "A Study of Schooling: Some Findings and Hypothesis," *Phi Delta Kappan*, March 1983, p. 467.
9. Sandy McKasson, *An Open Letter to Christian Parents and Teachers* (Dallas, Tex.: Educational Reform Foundation), p. 8.

SELECT
Bibliography

Adams, Jay. *Back to the Blackboard*. Phillipsburg, N.J.: Presbyterian and Reformed, 1982.

Blumenfeld, Samuel L. *How to Start Your Own Private School, and Why You Need One*. Boise, Idaho: Paradigm.

———. *How to Tutor*. Milford, Mich.: Mott Media, 1977.

———. *Is Public Education Necessary?* Boise, Idaho: Paradigm.

———. *NEA: Trojan Horse in American Education*. Boise, Idaho: Paradigm, 1984.

———. *The New Illiterates*. Boise, Idaho: Paradigm.

———. *The Retreat From Motherhood*. Boise, Idaho: Paradigm.

Byrne, H. W. *A Christian Approach to Education*. Milford, Mich.: Mott Media, 1977.

Chall, Jeanne. *Learning to Read: The Great Debate*. New York: McGraw-Hill, 1967.

Christian Liberty Academy. *Class Legal Manual*. Prospect Heights, Ill.: Christian Liberty Academy.

Copperman, Paul. *The Literacy Hoax*. New York: William Morrow and Co., 1978.

Damerell, Reginald G. *Education's Smoking Gun: How Teachers'*

Colleges Have Destroyed Education in America. New York: Freundlich Books, 1985.

De Jong, Norman. *Education in Truth*. Phillipsburg, N.J.: Presbyterian and Reformed, 1969.

Dobson, James. *Hide or Seek*. Expanded and updated ed. Old Tappan, N.J.: Revell, 1974.

Elkind, David. *The Hurried Child*. Reading, Pa.: Addison-Wesley, 1981.

Falwell, Jerry. *Listen America*. New York: Bantam.

Flesch, Rudolf. *Why Johnny Still Can't Read: A New Look at the Scandal of Our Schools*. New York: Harper & Row, 1983.

Foundation for American Christian Education. *The Bible and the Constitution of the United States of America*. San Francisco: Foundation for American Christian Education.

Fugate, J. Richard. *What the Bible Says About Child Training*. Tempe, Ariz.: Aletheia, 1980.

Gabler, Mel and Norma Gabler. *What Are They Teaching Our Children?* Wheaton, Ill.: Victor, 1985.

Hall, Verna M. *The Christian History of the Constitution of the United States of America*. San Francisco: Foundation for American Christian Education, 1960.

Holt, John. *Freedom and Beyond*. Boston, Mass.: Holt Associates, 1984.

———. *Teach Your Own: New and Hopeful Path for Parents and Educators*. New York: Delta, 1986.

Iserbyt, Charlotte. *Back to Basic Reform . . . or Skinnerian International Curriculum*. Upland, Calif.: Barbara Morris Report, 1985.

Kozol, Jonathan. *Illiterate America*. Garden City, N.Y.: Anchor Press, 1985.

LaHaye, Tim. *The Battle for the Mind*. Old Tappan, N.J.: Revell, 1983.

———. *The Battle for the Public Schools*. Old Tappan, N.J.: Revell, 1983.

Macaulay, Susan Schaeffer. *For the Children's Sake*. Westchester, Ill.: Crossway, 1984.

May, Phillip. *Which Way to Educate?* Chicago: Moody, 1975.

Moore, Raymond S., and Dorothy Moore. *Better Late Than Early*. New York: Readers' Digest Press.

———. *Home-grown Kids*. Waco, Tex.: Word, 1981.

———. *Homespun Schools*. Waco, Tex.: Word, 1982.

———. *Home-style Teaching*. Waco, Tex.: Word, 1984.

Nuttal, Clayton L. *The Conflict: The Separation of Church and State*. Schaumburg, Ill.: Regular Baptist Press, 1980.

Pride, Mary. *The Big Book of Home Learning*. Westchester, Ill.: Crossway, 1986.

————. *The Way Home: Beyond Feminism, Back to Reality*. Westchester, Ill.: Crossway, 1985.

Reed, Carl. *Our Reeds Grow Free*. Amarillo, Tex.: Owen Haney Press.

Reed, Sally. *NEA: Propaganda Front of the Radical Left*. Alexandria, Va.: NCBE, 1984.

Schaeffer, Francis A. *A Christian Manifesto*. Westchester, Ill.: Crossway, 1981.

Schindler, Claude, Jr. and Pacheo Pyle. *Educating for Eternity*. Wheaton, Ill.: Tyndale.

Schlafly, Phyllis, ed. *Child Abuse in the Classroom*. Alton, Ill.: Pere Marquette, 1984.

Slater, Rosalie J. *Teaching and Learning America's Christian History*. San Francisco: Foundation for American Christian Education, 1965.

Sommer, Carl. *Schools in Crisis: Training for Success or Failure?* 2nd ed. Houston, Tex.: Cahill, 1984.

Trumbull, H. Clay. *Hints on Child Training*. New York: Charles Scribner's Sons.

Vitz, Paul C. *Censorship: Evidence on Bias in Our Children's Textbooks*. Ann Arbor, Mich.: Servant, 1986.

Wade, Theodore E., Jr., et al. *The Home School Manual: For Parents Who Teach Their Own Children*. 2nd ed. Auburn, Calif.: Gazelle, 1986.

Whitehead, John W. *The Separation Illusion*. Milford, Mich.: Mott Media.

Whitehead, John W. and Wendell R. Bird. *Home Education and Constitutional Liberties*. Westchester, Ill.: Crossway, 1984.